SECOND EDITION

What Really Matters in Vocabulary

Research-Based Practices across the Curriculum

Patricia M. Cunningham

Wake Forest University

PEARSON

Boston   Columbus   Indianapolis   New York   San Francisco   Upper Saddle River
Amsterdam   Cape Town   Dubai   London   Madrid   Milan   Munich   Paris   Montreal   Toronto
Delhi   Mexico City   São Paulo   Sydney   Hong Kong   Seoul   Singapore   Taipei   Tokyo

Vice President, Editor-in-Chief: Aurora Martínez Ramos
Associate Sponsoring Editor: Barbara Strickland
Editorial Assistant: Katherine Wiley
Director of Marketing: Christine Gatchell
Project Manager: Maggie Brobeck
Text Designer: Denise Hoffman
Manager, Central Design: Jayne Conte

Cover Designer: Suzanne Behnke
Cover Art: AVAVA/Shutterstock
Full-Service Project Management and Composition:
Mahalatchoumy Saravanan/Jouve India Private Limited
Printer/Binder: Courier /Westford
Cover Printer: Courier/Westford
Text Font: Guardi LT Std 55 Roman 10.5/14.5 pt

Credits and acknowledgments borrowed from other sources and reproduced, with permission, in this textbook appear on the appropriate page within text or on this page.

Photo Credits: pp. 1, 3, 21, Dmitry/Shutterstock; pp. 7, 62, 109, 111, 147, Micromonkey/ Fotolia; pp. 10, 49, 53, 93, 144, 204, 221, Andriy/Fotolia; pp. 17, 19, Jacek Chabraszewski/Fotolia; pp. 30, 59, 125, Monkey Business Images/Shutterstock; pp. 33, 36, 170, 182, Pressmaster/Fotolia; pp. 43, 54, 81, 83, 207, StockLite/Shutterstock; pp. 46, 166, 209, 215, Yuri Arcurs/ Fotolia; pp. 56, 76, 177, 178, Petro Feketa/Fotolia; pp. 61, 199, 200, Oliveromg/Shutterstock; pp. 106, 153, 160, 187, 225, Michaeljung/Fotolia; pp. 115, 131, 135, Pressmaster/Shutterstock; pp. 52, 211, Patricia M. Cunningham.

Library of Congress Cataloging-in-Publication Data

Cunningham, Patricia Marr.
  What really matters in vocabulary : research-based practices across the curriculum / Patricia M. Cunningham. — Second edition.
    pages cm
  Includes bibliographical references and index.
  ISBN-13: 978-0-13-312445-3
  ISBN-10: 0-13-312445-2
 1. English language—Orthography and spelling—Study and teaching (Elementary)—United States. 2. English language—Orthography and spelling—Research—United States—Methodology. I. Title.
  LB1574.C88 2013
  372.44—dc23

2012050977

10 9 8 7 6 5 4 3 2 1

www.pearsonhighered.com

ISBN 10: 0-13-312445-2
ISBN 13: 978-0-13-312445-3

Contents

Preface

Vocabulary is a topic about which there is much talk and little action. Everyone knows that developing students' vocabularies is a critical goal in all subject areas, but the task seems so enormous that most of us don't know where to begin. Today, as in years past, the most common vocabulary activity in classrooms consists of having students look up words, copy definitions, put words in sentences, and learn the words for the vocabulary test. When asked, most of us acknowledge that these traditional vocabulary activities probably don't accomplish much. But what is the alternative? How do we increase the number of words students know meanings for as well as the depth of meanings for those words as a day-in, day-out, across-the-school-day priority?

I wrote this book to address the lack of vocabulary instruction in our elementary schools. I am concerned about all the students we teach, but I am most concerned about the ever-increasing number of students we teach who are not native English speakers and about children who live in economic poverty. The gap between the "haves" and "have-nots" in the United States affects all areas of schooling, but this gap is most apparent when looking at the differences in vocabulary—words students have meanings for and the depth of meanings they have for those words. In this book, I have gathered the most effective and "do-able" vocabulary instructional activities and provided examples and suggestions of how teachers can include these activities as they carry out instruction across the curriculum. I believe that if these activities are implemented "all day, every day," we can make progress in closing the wide vocabulary gap that exists in the United States today.

New to This Edition

In revising this book, I have tried to keep the focus on classroom and practical activities that teachers can use throughout the school day. I have incorporated examples from classrooms I have seen as I observe and supervise my student teachers. Every chapter in the book has been revised and updated. The most significant changes include:

- A new chapter on talk
- A new chapter on writing
- A new chapter on independent word learning
- More vocabulary-building activities for English language learners
- Incorporation of the Common Core State Standards for vocabulary
- Updated technology and other resources

Overview of Chapter Contents

Chapter 1 Why Vocabulary Matters

My purpose in Chapter 1 is to convince you that making an "all-day, every-day" commitment to maximizing vocabulary growth for all your students will result in increased learning in all the subjects you teach. Vocabulary words are the tools we use to understand and communicate what we are learning. Pronouncing words without knowing what the words mean and memorizing definitions cannot move our children forward in their reading or learning of content. Vocabulary is the foundation for learning. Increasing our emphasis on vocabulary will result in increases in achievement.

Chapter 2 Reading Is What Matters Most!

You learned most of the words in your meaning vocabulary store from your reading. The more you read, the bigger vocabulary you will have. The more your students read, the bigger vocabularies they will have. Chapter 2 describes classroom-tested strategies that will motivate all students to engage in more independent reading and ways to maximize the amount of vocabulary students learn during the daily teacher read-aloud time.

Chapter 3 Tell Your Students to Talk!

If all your instruction in a day were recorded, what do you think the ratio of teacher talk versus student talk would be? In most classrooms, the number of words spoken by the teacher is 10 to 20 times greater than the number of words spoken by all the children combined. Talking is one of the most common "behavior" problems teachers face, and yet students must use new words in talking if they are going to "own" the words. Chapter 3 suggests simple and quick ways to get students talking more—and talking about the things you want them to talk about.

Chapter 4 Writing Builds Expressive Vocabulary

Besides talking, writing is the other way you can help students add new words to their expressive vocabularies. Chapter 4 suggests ways to incorporate "quick-writes" into your instruction throughout the school day. These quick-writes allow you to give students "think time" and have been shown to increase both the quality and quantity of student thinking and learning.

Chapter 5 Teaching Vocabulary Independence

In order to learn new word meanings from their reading, students must notice a new word and think about what it means. Unfortunately, many children, when reading on their own, use the "skip it" strategy. They encounter an unfamiliar word, skip it, and continue reading. The meaning of most new words can be figured out if you use the clues from the surrounding text—the context—and word clues—familiar parts we call roots, prefixes, and suffixes. Informational text often includes pictures and other visuals that provide additional clues to the meanings of new words. Chapter 5 provides lesson templates you can use to model for your students how to use context, picture clues, and word-part clues to figure out the meanings of new words.

Chapter 6 Morpheme Magic

Morphemes are meaning units in words. The word *Internet* has two morphemes, the prefix *inter* and the root word *net*. *Blogger* has two morphemes, the root word *blog* and the suffix *er*. Linguists estimate that if you are morphologically sophisticated, you will understand how prefixes, suffixes, and roots work, and you will automatically figure out the meanings of six or seven words for every root word you know. If you know the meaning of *sign,* you should easily figure out what *signature, significant, insignificant, unsigned, signal,* and *cosign* mean. *Design, resign, designate,* and *resignation* are more possibilities if you are more morphologically sophisticated. Morphemes—the meaning building parts of words—are magic because they give you the power to instantly increase your vocabulary by hundreds, even thousands, of words. Chapter 6 provides detailed lesson plans for teaching the most useful prefixes, suffixes, and roots.

Chapter 7 Building Vocabulary While You Teach Reading

Introducing vocabulary before reading a selection is an everyday occurrence in most elementary classrooms. There are two reasons this vocabulary introduction is not apt to increase the number of vocabulary words most students know. First, in order for words to be added to vocabulary, students need to have several different encounters with the words across several days or weeks. Because the words being introduced for a selection are not likely to occur again in other selections, students do not have enough opportunities to encounter the words and make the words their own. The second reason much vocabulary instruction in reading lessons is not effective is because students (and teachers) think it's boring! Vocabulary introduction, putting words in sentences, and copying definitions is probably the biggest deterrent to students' developing word wonder! Chapter 7 describes engaging ways to maximize the effectiveness of vocabulary instruction during reading lessons.

Chapter 8 Building Vocabulary While You Teach Math

Each day, elementary children learn math, science, and social studies and participate in the arts and physical education. These academic content areas each have their own vocabularies, and the key words are used throughout the unit or sometimes across the entire year. Many experts suggest that most direct vocabulary instruction should take place in these academic content areas. Robert Marzano (2004), an advocate for the direct teaching of important vocabulary terms in all content areas, has developed an extensive list of 7,923 critical terms for all subjects K–12. Chapter 8 suggests a possible list of core elementary math vocabulary and provides you with practical activities you can incorporate so that your students will learn the math vocabulary and increase their achievement in math.

Chapter 9 Building Vocabulary While You Teach Science

Chapter 9 provides sample lists of core science vocabulary, along with specific vocabulary strategies for teaching the language of science. Strategies for making sure students have multiple and varied encounters with the words; for using real, concrete experiences and visuals to build meanings for words; and for getting children to use the words in talking and writing are described.

Chapter 10 Building Vocabulary While You Teach Social Studies

Social studies is an area of the curriculum where huge numbers of unfamiliar words reside. Many of these words are abstract concepts—*democracy, segregation, global*. This chapter includes sample lists of the academic vocabulary and concepts students need to understand and examples of lessons you can use to teach these words and concepts.

Chapter 11 Building Vocabulary While You Teach Art, Music, and PE

Most children love art, music, and PE. You can capitalize on their interest in these subjects to increase their vocabularies as they engage in hands-on, bodies-in concrete activities.

Chapter 12 Word Wonder

The final chapter of this book provides games, activities, and selected children's books that you can use to help your students develop their word consciousness and become "word people" who can't wait to encounter and befriend the next new word!

Book Study Guide for What Really Matters in Vocabulary

A book study guide is included with questions and suggestions for guiding the conversation about vocabulary. This guide helps study groups and professional learning communities assess the vocabulary instruction in their school and set priorities for vocabulary instruction across the curriculum.

Acknowledgments

The following reviewers provided helpful feedback for this edition: Erica Bowers, Ed.D, California State University at Fullerton; Dr. Pamela Godt, Western Illinois University; Amanda Grotting, Peavine Elementary School (Reno, NV); Leslie Hopping, Columbus Academy (Gahanna, OH); Erica D. McCray, Ph.D, University of Florida at Gainesville; and Kimberly Taylor-Gathings, Mississippi University for Women.

The What Really Matters *Series*

Dear Readers:

The Common Core State Standards (CCSS) adopted by almost all the states are bringing major changes to the way we conceptualize literacy instruction. The reading standards require students to read more difficult text and to use higher level thinking skills to make inferences and comparisons across texts. The listening, speaking, and language skills require students to develop discussion and critical listening skills. The writing standards require students to write narrative, persuasive, and informational pieces and to carry out research using multiple texts. The bar has been raised!

The "What Really Matters" series is designed to help you and your students meet these new standards. In this series, we bring you the best research-based instructional advice available. We have tried to cut through the research jargon and at least some of the messiness and provide plain-language guides for teaching students to read. Our main focus is helping you use the research as you plan and deliver reading lessons to your students. Together we will strive to help you make your lessons as effective as we know how, given the research that has been published.

Our goal, and we know it is yours, is that all children learn to enjoy and think critically about what they read, and write clearly and persuasively. Implementing the research-based and classroom-proven practices described in these books will help you assure that all your students can meet the higher standards and, more importantly, become active, engaged, and confident readers and writers.

So, enjoy these books and teach them all to read.

chapter 1

Why Vocabulary Matters

*M*eaning *vocabulary* is an intensely personal topic for me. The second year of my career found me teaching first grade in a large rural school 20 miles north of Tallahassee, Florida. All the children were bused to school from the surrounding plantations. Few if any parents ever came to school, having no way to get there.

On the first day of school, I looked out at 32 children left at my door by older brothers, sisters, and cousins. (Fortunately, these older children also gathered the first-graders from my classroom at the end of the day since neither my students nor I had any idea what bus they should ride!). At the end of the first day, I was supposed to send a "roll" of my students to the office. I knew I had 32 students, but I had only 29 names. Who were those other 3 children who had spent their first day of school in my classroom? (Florida had no public kindergarten at that time.) On the following morning, I put a name tag on all children as they came in the door, spelling their names as best I could. One child would not talk to me, and no one in the class seemed to know who he was. At the end of that day, I sent a roll with 31 names and one question mark. Needless to say, I was called to the office and ordered to supply the name of that student! The next morning, I stood at my door as the big kids dropped off the little ones. When I spotted the nameless child, I quickly nabbed his older brother and succeeded at getting a name to write on the name tag. Three days into the school year, I triumphantly sent a roll with names attached to all 32 of my students—although I had no confidence that I had spelled those names correctly!

Our school followed a very traditional curriculum. We had a math series with a workbook and a basal reading series with a six-week "readiness" program. I taught my children to count and recognize numbers. We learned letter names and sounds and auditory discrimination (very similar to what is now called phonemic awareness). The children were attentive and eager, and although no child knew these concepts before coming to school, some learned them remarkably fast. My biggest challenge and frustration was with their extremely limited vocabularies. This issue became obvious to me immediately because the readiness workbooks had page after page of pictures to which the children were supposed to attach beginning sounds. On a page with lots of **m** pictures, all the children could name the **man** and the **milk**. Some could name the **mop, moon, monkey,** and **motorcycle**. Everyone called the **mouse** a "rat." No one was able to name the **map, moose, mule,** or **mirror**. Math provided another daily example of my students' meager vocabulary stores. Most children understood the concept of counting and numbers such as 1, 2, and 3. Almost no one made any connections to ordinal numbers **first, second, third,** and so on. Position words were very frustrating for my first-graders. Most knew **over** and **under,** but **above, below, behind, left,** and **right** were simply not part of their vocabularies.

When I became aware of how meager the vocabularies of almost all my students were, I started making lists of words I needed to teach. Knowing that the best way to teach words was with real objects, I raided my apartment and the apartments of my friends and carted in objects whenever I could. As I began to gather the objects, I realized that one example object is almost never enough. My mop at home was the squeeze type; the mop pictured in the readiness book was a "stringy" mop. The mirror I took off my wall at home bore little resemblance to the hand-held mirror pictured. Having a concept for "mop" and "mirror" was clearly much broader than any one example. Many words could not be represented by objects, so I found my picture file, assiduously collected during all my undergraduate education courses. This was of some help, but I had not a single picture of a motorcycle, mule, or moose! I haunted yard sales, grabbing old magazines and encyclopedias, and expanded my picture file. (I could never have imagined at that time being able to download and print images from Google!)

Each time I tried to build concepts for words on my list, I discovered more words my students didn't know. **Moose** live in **herds** and have **antlers**. A **mule** is part **donkey** and has **hooves**. What you see in the **mirror** is your **reflection**. Sometimes the **moon** is **full** and sometimes it is a **half** or **quarter** moon. (I am sure I did not convince some of my children that there actually is *not* a man in the moon!)

Another complication in my attempt to build meaning vocabularies became evident when a child announced that Jackson didn't come to school today because he got "bus left." "That's right," confirmed another child. Since I had diligently been working on the concepts of "left" and "right"—left hand, right hand, left side, right side—I recognized other entirely different meanings for these words. Once I became aware of how many common words had two or more very different meanings, these multimeaning words were everywhere! The lines on their handwriting paper had little to do with the lines we formed to go to the playground. Being second in line had little to do with the 60 seconds in a minute. The letters we were trying so hard to learn names and sounds for were not like the letters received from grandmothers and aunts. There was also confusion with words that are spelled differently but sound exactly the same to children who are just learning the word meanings.

"Were you the **one** who **won** the race?"

"The coach **blew** the **blue** whistle."

"Yesterday we **read** the **red** book."

Every day, the list of vocabulary I needed to teach grew longer and longer as new words, words connected to previous words, multimeaning words, and homophones were added. Finally, the list got so long that I gave up! I realized that I would never be able to teach directly all the words my students needed. But I worried. How were they ever going to learn them?

I gave up writing the words on the list, but I did not give up the constant day-in and day-out battle to increase the size of the children's meaning vocabularies. To build their vocabularies, I relied on three activities: reading to the children, using a wide variety of visuals, and studying real objects.

I read to the children every day from picture books and used the pictures in the books as opportunities for vocabulary development. I discovered that pictures not only worked for nouns but could also help me build other concepts. When a character in a book was angry, we talked about (and mimicked) the expression on that character's face. We also came up with other words for angry such as **mad** and **furious**. A few weeks later, when Rumpelstiltskin flew into a rage when the queen guessed his name, we concluded that when you "fly into a rage," you are really angry, mad, and furious. I also used pictures to teach describing words. For example, I would ask the students to tell by looking at a picture whether the weather was cloudy, sunny, or rainy. Reading a picture book about animals, we talked about how the animals moved, and later, on the playground, we galloped, hopped, and scampered.

I continued to scavenge everywhere for pictures to add to my picture file, and I also found some filmstrips that connected to some of our science and social studies topics. On special occasions, I took some Polaroid photographs of the children doing various activities and labeled and posted these. (I never imagined at that time what could be done with a digital camera!) My best teaching friend, Elaine, taught second grade across the hall, and she occasionally got movies from the Tallahassee public library. We crowded both our classes into her classroom, popped popcorn, and had a movie party. We stopped the movie regularly and asked the question the children were now familiar with: "Do you know what we call this?" This was a very special treat for the students, most of whom did not have televisions and almost none of whom had ever gone to a movie.

The third daily staple of our vocabulary-building diet was real objects. The children and I named every single thing in the room, including the parts of things: "Doors have knobs and hinges. What else has knobs? Hinges?" "The part around the door is the frame. What other kinds of frames do you see in the room?" Each day, the children left with an assignment to see whether they could find the things we named in our classroom at home. To their delight, all the children discovered that their houses had doors, knobs, hinges, and frames! When we had about exhausted naming the things in our classroom, we branched out to the cafeteria, the auditorium, the office (on a day when the principal, who was less than sympathetic, was at a staff meeting downtown). Next, we took "naming walks" outside the school. We named trees and parts of trees—branches, leaves, roots, bark, and so on. One of the children realized that dogs bark, too, and everyone tried to think of other words with multiple meanings.

> "The **leaves** on the trees are not like when you **leave** somewhere."
>
> "There are **rocks** here, and you can **rock** in a **rocking** chair."
>
> "And **rock** music, and you can **rock** around the clock!"

Unfortunately, there were many things not available in our school environment and for which pictures were not particularly helpful. Our basal reading series featured two suburban children, Janet and Mark, and their dog, Socks. The stories were quite appealing but often had the children going places that my students could not even imagine. In one story, the children in the reader went to a department store and rode the escalator. Imagine trying to explain an escalator to children whose concept of stairs is the three steps going up to their porch! In another story, the textbook characters went to the park, sailed boats in a pond, and rode on the seesaw. Also, Janet and Mark went with their grandparents to a restaurant and ordered food from the menu, which is brought to them by the waitress. I doubt that any of my students had been to a park or a restaurant. Building concepts and vocabulary for the selections in our basal reader was a daily source of frustration for me.

As the year was coming to a close, Elaine and I connived to take our children on a fieldtrip to Tallahassee, which was 25 minutes away and to which almost none of the children had ever been. It was not easy, but we corralled a school bus to take us, and the cafeteria packed lunches for everyone. Somehow, we got permission slips signed and returned, and on a hot Thursday in May, we boarded the bus and headed to the big city! We began in a department store and spent quite a long time riding up and down the escalator. We didn't eat in a restaurant, but we did walk through and observe the menus and waitresses. We had lunch in the park, where we sailed boats in the pond and rode on a seesaw. The next day, we reread the stories in which Janet and Mark rode the escalator in the department store, lunched in a restaurant, and played in the park. "Better late than never," I thought as the children finally comprehended and connected to what they were reading in the book.

I hope the children learned as much from me that year as I learned from them. Like most teachers, I did my best, but I knew my best was not good enough. From that early teaching experience, I learned firsthand how much meaning vocabulary matters and how complex it is to teach children meanings for words.

In many ways, things are better today in schools for children who used to be called "underprivileged" and "disadvantaged." Every state now has public kindergarten and pre-K available for children who need it most. The Web and other technologies make "bringing words to life" a richer and more obtainable goal. As I write this, teachers still have many children coming to school with impoverished vocabularies. Many of these children come from poor families and many do not come with much English. Using every available resource to build rich meaning vocabularies for these children is key to ensuring their success in school and in life.

Vocabulary Affects Reading Comprehension

A large body of research indicates that vocabulary knowledge is positively related to comprehension (Lehr, Osborn, & Hiebert, 2004). There is also evidence that vocabulary instruction positively affects comprehension (Baumann, Kamene'enui, & Ash, 2003). There is no way to overstate the importance of meaning vocabulary to comprehension. The size of a person's vocabulary is one of the best predictors of how well he or she will comprehend while listening or reading. Simply stated, having a bigger vocabulary makes you a better reader.

How Many Words?

How many words do you know?

5,000?
10,000?
20,000?
50,000?
100,000?

If you found it difficult to estimate the size of your vocabulary, you should be comforted to know that this seemingly "simple" question of how many words you know is a difficult one to answer. The first issue is, of course, what is meant by "know." Is it enough to know that **anthropoids** are some kind of ape, or do you have to have the specific information that anthropoids are apes without tails, such as chimpanzees, gorillas, orangutans, and gibbons? The next question is how many meanings of the word do you have to know? If you know the sports meaning of **coach,** do you also have to know the motorbus and "coach class" meanings to count this word in your meaning vocabulary? The other complication in counting words you have meanings for is how you count the various forms of a word. If **work, works, worked, working, worker, workout, workbook, unworkable,** and **workroom** count as separate words, your vocabulary is much larger than if these words count as one word, all related to the root word **work.**

All these variables—word depth, multimeaning words, and how to count words with the same root—result in wide differences in the estimate of vocabulary size. In spite of the difficulties of estimating vocabulary size, it is important for teachers to have an idea of what the meaning vocabulary development goal is. Biemiller (2004) estimates that entering kindergartners have meanings for an average of 3,500 root words. They add approximately 1,000 root word meanings each school year. The average high school graduate knows about 15,000 root words.

Other vocabulary experts (Graves, 2006; Stahl & Nagy, 2006) argue that Biemiller's estimate is way too low. They believe that words with multiple meanings should be counted as separate words and that many children do not recognize words with common roots. Furthermore, they believe that proper nouns—such as Canada, Abraham Lincoln, and London—should be included in the total word count. When counted in this way, these experts argue that the average child learns 2,000 to 3,000 word meanings each school year and that the average high school graduate has meanings for 40,000 to 50,000 words. Regardless of which estimates you accept, the number of new words children need to add to their vocabularies each year is staggering.

Children differ greatly, however, in the size of their meaning vocabularies at school entrance and as they continue through the grades. These differences in vocabulary size are not random but rather are closely related to socioeconomic status. In 1995, Hart and Risley found that children of professional parents were exposed to 50 percent more words than children from working-class homes. When compared to children in families receiving Aid to Families with Dependent Children, children of professional parents were exposed to twice as many words. Hart and Risley concluded that children from the most affluent homes had vocabularies five times as large as children from the lowest-income homes and that the most important difference in families was the amount of talking that went on. The gap in meaning vocabulary begins early and often continues to widen as children move through school.

Another group of students who come to school with much smaller than average meaning vocabularies are children whose first language is not English. Cummins (1994) states that although children whose first language is not English can often develop fluency in conversational English in a year or two, it takes five or more years for children to bridge the gap and become fluent in the academic English required to succeed in all areas of the school curriculum.

Another reason that the size of a child's meaning vocabulary is crucial to school success is that vocabulary knowledge is cumulative. The more words you know at any point in time, the more words you are able to add to your vocabulary. Shefelbine (1990) investigated children's ability to infer meanings of words from context. Many children with limited vocabularies could not use context clues to figure out meanings for new words because they lacked meanings for many of the words that comprised the context! Children who enter school with small vocabularies tend to add fewer words each year than children who enter with larger vocabularies.

How Do We Learn All Those Words?

To help you understand how we add words to our meaning vocabulary stores, consider the analogy that learning word meanings is a lot like getting to know people. As with words, you know some people extremely well, you are acquainted with others, and you have only vague ideas of still others. Knowledge of people depends on the experiences you have with them. You know some people, such as family members and close friends, extremely well because you have spent most of your life in their company. You have participated with them regularly in situations that have been intense and emotional as well as routine. At the other extreme, think of people that you have only heard about, as well as historical figures such as Charles Darwin and Catherine the Great and current public figures such as politicians and entertainers. You have heard of them and seen pictures and videos of them, but these people are known only through the secondhand reports of others. Your knowledge of people that you know indirectly through secondhand information is limited in comparison to those you know directly through firsthand experience. Learning words—like coming to know people—varies according to how much time you spend with them and the types of experiences you share.

Now think of how you make new friends. Social gatherings such as parties and meetings are excellent opportunities for getting to know others. When you move through a gathering on your own, you strike up conversations and get to know new people in part as a function of your motivation and your social skills. However, having a host, hostess, or friend introduce you to people tends to expedite the process. Then, once you have made new contacts, you might get to know those individuals better as you meet again in other settings. And don't forget the power of social networking: The more people you know, the more opportunities you have for helping each other out and meeting even more people.

Are you a "people person"? Do you know someone whom you would describe as a "people person"? A people person is someone who genuinely likes people and finds them fascinating. A people person is always seeking out new individuals and making new friends. Of course, a people person knows a lot more people than those of us who are a little shyer and more reserved.

Levels of knowledge about people and the dynamics of getting to know them are comparable in many ways to learning words. When given the opportunity, students learn new words on their own, depending on their motivation and literacy skills. Students also benefit from direct introductions and intensive interactions with some new words. As students learn new words, their opportunities for learning additional words increase exponentially. Some students are "word people." They enjoy encountering a new word and are eager to add interesting words to their vocabularies. When they meet a new word, they think about how it is different from other words they know and are eager to try out this new word in discussions with their friends. This fascination with new words is often called "word consciousness" or "word wonder." Students who have so-called word wonder get to know a lot more words—just as a people person knows a lot more people.

Seven Principles for Maximizing Your Students' Vocabularies

Literacy experts agree on the need for vocabulary building for all students in all subjects and in all grades. There has been a lot of disagreement, however, about the best way to provide students with the valuable vocabulary tools they need. Some experts argue that since students need to learn so many new words each year, and since we cannot possibly teach 1,000 to 3,000 new words well, we would be better off spending our time teaching students how to learn words independently from their reading and providing time and encouragement for large amounts of independent reading. Other experts argue that when words are thoroughly taught, they do increase comprehension of text containing those words, and therefore direct teaching of vocabulary is important even though the number of words we can reasonably teach well is limited.

Everyone agrees that developing in all students a sense of word wonder will result in increased vocabulary learning. Because independent learning of vocabulary, direct teaching of selected words, and developing word wonder all contribute to vocabulary growth, students who are lucky enough to experience quality instruction in all three approaches are apt to develop the largest vocabularies. Thus, as in so many other areas of the elementary curriculum, we must "roll up our sleeves" and do it all. To be effective, vocabulary development has to be an "all day, every day" pervasive part of the curriculum. Rather than having a separate vocabulary period, we must weave rich vocabulary instruction in all that we do. This book presents a comprehensive vocabulary framework for the elementary classroom. This framework is based on the following seven principles:

1. Vocabulary is learned best when it is based on real, concrete experiences.

2. Pictures and other visuals help solidify word meanings.

3. To truly own a word, you must use that word in talking and writing.

4. A set of essential words, including academic subject-area vocabulary, should be directly taught.

5. Because most new words are learned through reading, teacher read-aloud and independent reading time should be scheduled into every elementary student's day.

6. Students should be taught strategies for learning new words independently from reading, including instruction in word parts, context, and effective use of the dictionary.

7. Instruction should include activities that develop word wonder and exclude ineffective, de-motivating activities such as copying and memorizing definitions and writing vocabulary words in sentences.

Vocabulary and English Language Learners

The number of students in our schools whose first language is not English continues to grow every year. From the 1997–98 school year, the number of English language learners enrolled in public schools increased by 51 percent, from 3.5 million to 5.3 million; during the same period, the general population of students grew by 7.2 percent (National Clearinghouse for English Language Acquisition, 2011). The U.S. Census Bureau (2010) estimates that by the year 2030, 40 percent of school-aged students will speak a language other than English. Of all English language learners, approximately 80 percent are Spanish speaking. Almost every teacher now teaches students who are learning English as they are mastering all the other goals of the elementary school curriculum. Obviously, these children come with smaller English vocabularies, and their limited vocabularies affect their learning in all subject areas. Throughout this book, suggestions are included for boosting the meaning vocabularies of your English language learners.

Vocabulary and the Common Core State Standards

Almost all the states have adopted a set of common standards for English/Language Arts and Mathematics. These Common Core State Standards (2010)* specify what students in grades 1 through 12 need to learn and be able to do. Strategies for acquiring new vocabulary and using vocabulary in all subject areas pervade these standards. Look at these standards from grade 5 and think about the sophisticated vocabulary strategies all fifth-graders are expected to apply. Reading Standard 4 requires fifth-graders to be able to:

- Determine the meaning of words and phrases as they are used in a text, including figurative language such as metaphors and similes.
- Determine the meaning of general academic and domain-specific words and phrases in a text relevant to a grade 5 topic or subject area.

Language Standards 4, 5, and 6 require fifth-graders to be able to:

- Determine the meaning of unknown and multimeaning words and phrases based on grade 5 reading and content, choosing flexibly from a range of strategies.
  - Use context as a clue to the meaning of a word or a phrase.

© Copyright 2010. National Governors Association Center for Best Practices and Council of Chief State School Officers. All rights reserved.

- Use common, grade-appropriate Greek and Latin affixes and roots as a clue to the meaning of a word or phrase.
- Consult reference materials, both print and digital, to find the pronunciation and determine or clarify the precise meaning of key words and phrases.
- Demonstrate understanding of figurative language, word relationships, and nuances in word meanings.
  - Interpret figurative language, including similes and metaphors, in context.
  - Recognize and explain the meaning of common idioms, adages, and proverbs.
- Use the relationship between particular words to better understand each of the words.
- Acquire and use accurately grade-appropriate general academic and domain-specific words and phrases, including those that signal contrast, addition, and other logical relationships.

Writing standards 1, 2, and 3 also demonstrate the crucial part vocabulary plays in students' literacy development. Fifth-graders need to demonstrate that they can:

- Write opinion pieces and link opinions and reasoning using words, phrases, and clauses (e.g, consequently, specifically).
- Write informational pieces in which they use precise language and domain-specific vocabulary to inform or explain the topic and link ideas within categories of information using words, phrases, and clauses (e.g., in contrast, especially).
- Write narratives in which they use concrete words and phrases and sensory details to convey experiences and events precisely and use a variety of transitional words, phrases, and clauses to manage the sequence of events.

Helping all our students build large, deep, and precise vocabularies should be a major goal of all teachers because words are the building blocks for comprehension and communication. It is simply the right thing to do. It is also the pragmatic thing to do because passing the Common Core assessments will not be possible without these rich vocabularies. Often we teachers have to make a choice between teaching our students what they need and what will help them pass the tests. When it comes to vocabulary, we don't have to make that choice. A day-in, day-out, across-the-curriculum emphasis on vocabulary will result in our students being better thinkers and communicators and achieving passing scores on these high-stakes tests.

Research Support for a Comprehensive Vocabulary Program

Most research studies of vocabulary instruction are short-term interventions focused on one particular aspect of vocabulary. Often these studies are conducted in a laboratory rather than a classroom setting. A study published in the October 2007 issue of *The Reading Teacher* (Baumann, Ware, & Carr Edwards) was conducted in a fifth-grade classroom across the entire school year and measured the effect of a comprehensive vocabulary development program. The study was carried out in a diverse low-income school in which 65 percent of the students qualified for free or reduced-price lunch. The multifaceted vocabulary program was modeled on that outlined by Graves (2006) and included the four components he identified as effective:

1. Providing rich and varied language experiences

2. Teaching individual words

3. Teaching word learning (morphology, context, dictionary) strategies

4. Fostering word consciousness

The article includes a rich description of the classroom instruction that assured students were engaged in vocabulary learning consisting of all four components. To provide rich and varied language experiences, the teacher read to the students daily and focused on the vivid vocabulary found in the rich literature. During their daily independent reading time, students recorded "new, interesting, and unusual" words they found in their reading. Weekly dialogue journals provided the teacher an opportunity to support and encourage students' discovery of new words in their reading. The use of "strong words" was also modeled and encouraged as students engaged in daily writing workshops.

To teach individual words, the teacher relied heavily on a vocabulary wall to which students and teacher added interesting words. Students also did self-assessments of how well they knew key words chosen by the teacher before reading selections and then worked with these words using a variety of graphic organizers and other activities that required students to categorize words and determine shades of meaning. The teaching of individual words occurred as part of the regular reading instruction and instruction in all curriculum areas.

Word learning strategy instruction included lessons on common prefixes, suffixes, and roots, and students were encouraged to add example words to a class chart. Instruction on various types of context clues and how to use a dictionary to clarify the meaning of a word was also included throughout the year.

Word consciousness was fostered as students engaged in a variety of word-play activities and sought out instances of metaphorical and figurative language. For one activity designed to enhance word consciousness, students interviewed parents and grandparents to discover what kind of slang was used by previous generations and created a class chart of old slang, including "toodle-loo" for good-bye and "been there, done that" for something already experienced.

To determine the effectiveness of this yearlong, comprehensive vocabulary program, students' vocabularies were measured at the beginning and end of the year using both receptive and expressive vocabulary instruments. In addition, students completed assessments designed to measure their interest in vocabulary, and parents indicated how often their students talked about learning new vocabulary.

At the end of the year, students demonstrated vocabulary growth on both quantitative and qualitative measures. Their expressive (speaking) vocabularies grew more than expected in one year's time. Their receptive (listening) vocabularies also grew, and this growth was greater for students who started the year with smaller receptive vocabularies. A comparison of writing samples from the beginning and end of the year indicated that students used 36 percent more words and 42 percent more low-frequency words in their end-of-the-year writing sample. Qualitative results indicated that students' aptitude toward learning new words increased, as did their ability to use word-learning strategies and their willingness to engage in word play.

I end this introductory chapter with this description of a yearlong classroom study of multifaceted vocabulary instruction in the hopes that it will inspire you as it has inspired me. It is logical to believe that a comprehensive program of vocabulary development across the curriculum will improve vocabulary, and this study provides evidence of its effectiveness. It is important to keep in mind that the fifth-graders in this classroom were mostly from low-income homes—the very students most affected by the vocabulary gap. There is no simple or quick fix for increasing the size and depth of students' vocabularies. As you read and think about how to implement a comprehensive across-the-curriculum vocabulary program in your classroom, have confidence that your efforts will reap rich rewards!

chapter 2

Reading Is What Matters Most!

Before children come to school, they learn new word meanings primarily from their language interactions with others. Once they come to school, they are given daily instruction that includes word

meanings. Kindergartners participate in daily calendar activities and learn the names of the days of the weeks and the months. In October, they learn the names of the seasons and words associated with fall. As they continue through the primary grades, they acquire science, math, and social studies words as they learn about animals, measurement, and holidays.

As children continue through the upper elementary grades, middle school, and high school, they continue to learn words they are directly taught, but most of the 2,000 to 3,000 words the average student gains from third grade on are learned from reading. The research summarized by Baumann (2009) indicates that wide reading is the major contributor to individual differences in vocabulary size.

To demonstrate how we learn most new word meanings from third grade on, consider the research of Hayes and Ahrens (1988). They analyzed the words that people encounter in a variety of oral language contexts, including adult speech and television programs, and print resources such as newspapers, magazines, children's and adult books, and comic books. They concluded that all types of print resources—including children's books and comic books—contained more rare words than any of the oral language situations. Children are much more likely to encounter words not in their current vocabularies when they are reading or being read to than when they engage or listen to conversations.

The number of words in your meaning vocabulary store is directly related to how much you read. Children who read the most have the biggest vocabularies. Children who read only when they are assigned something to read have smaller vocabularies.

Children who like to read and are good readers read much more than children who don't like to read and who struggle with reading. This connection between how well you read, how much you read, and vocabulary size is well known, but its implications for daily classroom life are often ignored. Many teachers just accept the fact that their struggling readers don't like to read and that they avoid reading whenever possible. Because of the clear relationship between meaning vocabulary size and volume of reading, accepting the idea that "some kids just don't like to read" means those kids will never become good readers.

There is a vicious cycle here that begins when children come to school with few print experiences and small meaning vocabularies. These children struggle with learning to read. Because reading is hard for them, they avoid reading. But since reading is one of the major ways new words are learned, the meaning vocabulary gap between children who like to read and read well and children who struggle with reading grows wider every day. Children who come to school with rich meaning vocabularies read more and add more words to their vocabularies. Children who come to school with impoverished meaning vocabularies read less and add fewer words. If there is any hope of truly "closing the gap" in literacy, we must all commit ourselves to making reading something all our students enjoy and choose. Children cannot all read at the same level, but they can all learn to find pleasure in reading.

What can you do to create a whole class of children who like to read? The answer to that question is simple and straightforward. You read to children every day from a wide variety of books, magazines, and newspapers. You provide time every day for children to read whatever they choose to read. You provide access to the widest possible range of reading materials. You arrange for regular opportunities for children to share what they are reading with you and with their friends.

Assess and Document Your Students' Independent Reading

If having all your students reading more and with greater enthusiasm is one of your most important goals, you are more likely to achieve that goal if you know where your students are early in the year and how they are progressing toward that goal during the year. Many teachers do a "status" assessment early in the year to determine how children feel about themselves as readers. They file these away and then have the children respond to the same questions halfway through the year and at the end of the year. After the children assess themselves halfway through the year, give them the report they completed early in the year and have them compare how they are "growing up" as readers. File both the early report and the midyear report. At the end of the year, have children self-report their reading habits one last time. After completing the final report, give them the first and second reports and have them write a paragraph summarizing their change and growth as readers.

Me and Reading

My name is _____.

Here is how I feel about reading as of _____(today's date).

The best book I ever read is _____.

I like it because _____.

The best book I read in the last 4 months is _____.

I like it because _____.

My favorite author is _____.

My favorite kind of book is _____.

When I am home, I read: (Circle one)

Almost never   Sometimes   Almost every day   Every day

This is how I feel about reading right now: (Circle one)

I love reading.   I like reading OK.   I don't like reading.   I hate reading.

Many children are amazed (and proud!) to see how much more they like to read. The Me and Reading form is one example of the type of questions you might use to help you and your students assess their growth as readers.

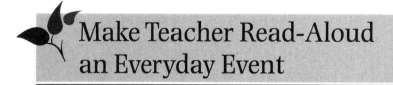

Make Teacher Read-Aloud an Everyday Event

Teacher read-aloud is a proven method for increasing children's desire to read. In 1975, Sterl Artley asked successful college students what they remembered their teachers doing that motivated them to read. The majority of students responded that they got interested in reading when teachers read aloud to the class. More recently, elementary students were asked what motivated them to read particular books. The most frequent response was "My teacher read it to the class" (Palmer, Codling, & Gambrell, 1994). Ivey and Broaddus (2001) surveyed 1,765 sixth-graders to determine what motivated them to read. This large group of diverse preteens indicated that having time for independent reading of books of their own choosing and having teachers read aloud to them were most motivating.

Reading aloud to children is a simple and research-proven way to motivate children of all ages to become readers. When thinking about your struggling readers, however, you need also to consider what you are reading aloud. Did you know that most of the fiction sold in bookstores is sold to women and most of the informational books are sold to men? Now this doesn't mean that women never read informational texts or that men never read fiction, it just means that there does seem to be a preference among males for information.

Reading aloud stimulates motivation, and what we read aloud may really matter to struggling readers. In *True Stories from Four Blocks Classrooms,* Deb Smith (2001) describes her daily teacher read-aloud session. Each day, Deb reads one chapter from a fiction book, a part of an informational book, and an "everyone" book. She chooses the "everyone" book by looking for a short, simple book that "everyone in my class will enjoy and can read." (She *never* calls these books easy books.) By reading from these three types of books daily, Deb demonstrates to her students that all kinds of books are cherished and acceptable in her classroom. Deb follows her teacher read-aloud with independent reading time. The informational books and the "everyone" books are popular choices—especially with her boys who struggle with reading.

Reading aloud to students is more common in primary grades than in upper grades, even though it might be more important for teachers of older children to read aloud. Most children develop the reading habit between the ages of 8 and 11. Reading aloud to older children provides the motivation for them to read at the critical point when they have the literacy skills to take advantage of that motivation. Teachers of older children can show them the whole range of what adults read by bringing real-world reading materials such as newspapers and magazines into the classroom and reading tidbits from these with an "I was reading this last night, and I just couldn't wait to get here and share it with you" attitude. Intermediate teachers need to make a special effort to read books from all the different sections of the bookstore. Most of us who are readers established our reading preferences in those preteen years. If we read *Cam Jansen* mysteries then, we probably still enjoy reading mysteries today. If we read *Star Wars* and *Star Trek* books then, we probably still enjoy science fiction today. If we packed biographies of famous people and informational books about sports to take to camp, the books we pack in our vacation travel bag today are probably still more information than fiction.

One way you can motivate more of your students to become readers is to read some books in a series and some books by authors who have written lots of other books. Remember that your students often want to read the book you read aloud. Read aloud one of David Adler's *Cam Jansen* mysteries and then show your students several more Cam Jansen mysteries that you "wish you had time to read aloud to them." Read aloud one of Gail Gibbons's informational books on animals—perhaps *Sharks* or *Whales* or *Dogs*—and then show the children the other 40 you "wish you had time to read to them." Your students who like mysteries may have "choice anxiety" trying to decide which *Cam Jansen* mystery to read first, and your animal-lover informational readers will not know where to begin with all of Gail Gibbons's wonderful animal books. Unlike most anxiety, this kind of choice anxiety is a good thing!

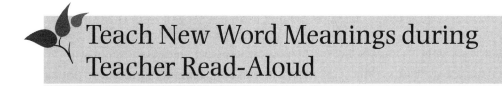

Teach New Word Meanings during Teacher Read-Aloud

Teacher read-aloud is one of the major opportunities for your students to learn new word meanings. You can increase the number of new words children learn from your read-aloud by stopping occasionally to focus on an interesting or unusual word or phrase. Imagine that the sentence you have just read is:

> The players were tossing the ball to one another to limber up their muscles before the game.

Pause and ask your students what they think "limber up their muscles" means. Let your sports enthusiasts explain what players do before games to "limber" up their muscles, make a quick connection between arms and legs being called "limbs," and proceed with your reading.

Or perhaps in a book about a volcano there is a picture of all the residents fleeing their town and the sentence:

> Everyone evacuated as quickly as possible, cramming all they could fit into their packed vehicles.

Use this picture and rich context to help students add the word "evacuated" to their vocabularies. If you seize the opportunity to focus briefly on unfamiliar words as you read aloud, not only will you be helping students add words to their vocabularies but you will be modeling how we use context and pictures and sometimes familiar word parts (limb–limber) to learn new words from our reading.

Another way to be intentional in fostering vocabulary development through your teacher read-aloud is to choose some books specifically for their vocabulary development potential. For young children, alphabet books with just a few words and clear illustrations for each word can greatly increase the size of their vocabularies while simultaneously teaching them important letter–name, letter–sound, and phonemic awareness concepts. Using the colorful illustrations in John Burningham's *ABC*, children can build meanings for words including *clown, elephant, iguana, jungle, lion, mice, king, queen, tractor,* and *volcano.* The illustrations in Max Grover's *The Accidental Zucchini* can help build meaning for *canyon, elevator, goldfish, railroad, sailor, tuba,* and *yard.*

In addition to alphabet books, simple and clearly illustrated concept books help children add words and meanings to their vocabularies. Roger Priddy has a whole series of concept books, including *Opposites; Colors; Shapes;* and *My Big World.* Nancy Coffelt's *Big, Bigger, Biggest!* and *Aunt Ant Leaves through the Leaves* help children learn synonyms for common words and how words that sound the same can have very different meanings. Sandra Boynton is another author of concept books, including *Horns to Toes and in Between; One, Two, Three!;* and *The Going to Bed Book.* Children love the Richard Scarry books, including *Cars and Trucks and Things That Go; A Day at the Airport;* and *A Day at the Fire Station.*

With both alphabet books and concept books, it is important to read the books to the children several times. On the first reading, read the book and encourage them to talk about what they see in the pictures. On the second reading, have children predict what pictures and words they will see before

ABC and Concept Books Are Perfect for Your English Language Learners

Including clearly illustrated alphabet and concept books in your teacher read-aloud will increase the meaning vocabularies for all your students, but it is crucial for your English language learners. Most children who are learning English have the concepts illustrated in these books—they just don't know the English word that goes with the concept. Have your ELLs tell their talking partner what the word in their first language is for the various pictures. Be sure to assign your ELLs an empathetic talking partner who will support and encourage them as they attempt to use the English words. Using new words in speech is important for all children in learning those words, but speaking the words is essential for children learning English. Alphabet and simple concept books are appropriate read-alouds for all young children including ELLs. These same books are also a wonderful source for vocabulary development in teaching older children who are just beginning to learn English.

turning each page. To get more children speaking more words, seat your children with "talking partners" and ask them to talk together. Before you turn each page, they can tell their partners what they think will be on that page. After you read a page, ask them to talk with their partners about their experience with the words pictured. For example, you might say, "Talk to your partner about what you do on a rainy day when you are at home."

Make Time Every Day for Independent Reading

The goal of every elementary teacher should be to have all children reading for at least 20 minutes each day from materials they have chosen to read. Use an analogy to help your children understand that becoming good at reading is just like becoming good at anything else. Compare learning to read with learning to play the piano, tennis, or baseball. Explain that in order to become good at anything, you need three things: (1) instruction, (2) practice on the skills, and (3) practice on the whole thing. To become a good tennis player, you need to (1) take tennis lessons, (2) practice the skills (backhand, serve, etc.), and (3) play tennis. To become a good reader, you also need instruction, practice on the important skills, and practice reading. Point out that sometimes we get so busy that we may forget to take the important time each day to read; therefore, we must schedule it just like anything else we do.

Although at least 20 minutes daily for independent reading is the goal, you may want to start with a shorter period of time and increase the time gradually as children establish the reading habit and learn to look forward to this daily "read what you want to" time. Some teachers use a timer to signal the beginning and end of the independent reading time. When we engage in activities regularly, we establish some natural time rhythms. Using a timer to monitor the independent reading time helps children establish these rhythms. When the timer sounds at the end of the session, you should probably say something like, "Take another minute if you need to get to a good stopping point."

Once the time for independent reading begins, do not allow your students to move around the room looking for something to read. Some teachers have children choose several pieces of reading material before the time begins and do not allow children to get up and change material until the time ends. In other classrooms, teachers place a crate of books on each table, and children can choose from that crate. The book crates rotate from table to table every few days so that all the children have access to lots of different books "within arm's length."

Establishing and enforcing the "no wandering" rule is particularly important for struggling readers. If children have not been successful with reading in the past and they are allowed to move around the room to look for books during the independent reading time, they are very apt to spend more time wandering than reading. Remember that one of your major reasons for committing yourself to this daily independent reading time is that you know that how much the children read plays a critical role in how well they read. If your good readers read for almost all the allotted time and your struggling readers read for only half the time, the gap between your good and poor readers will further widen as the year goes on. Having a good variety of materials "within arm's reach" is crucial if struggling readers are going to profit from this precious time you are setting aside each day for independent reading.

If you begin with just five or six minutes, kindergartners and early first-graders can engage in independent reading even before they can read. Think about your own children or young children you have known. Young children who have been read to regularly often look at their books and pretend they are reading. Kindergartners and early first-graders should be encouraged to get in the habit of reading even before they can do it. Many teachers of young children prompt with, "Pretend that you are the teacher and you are reading the book." Kindergarten children are also very motivated to read if they are allowed to select a stuffed animal or a doll to read to.

Accumulate the Widest Possible Variety of Reading Materials

For successful independent reading, it is crucial that students choose their own reading materials and have a variety of materials from which to choose. Collecting lots of appealing books requires determination, cleverness, and an eye for bargains. In addition to obvious sources such as free books you get from book clubs when your students order books, asking parents to donate, begging for books from your friends and relatives whose children have outgrown them, and haunting yard sales and thrift shops, there are some less obvious sources as well. Libraries often sell or donate used books and magazines on a regular basis. Some bookstores will give you a good deal on closeouts and may even set up a "donation basket" where they will collect used books for you. (Take some pictures of your eager readers and have your children write letters telling what kind of books they like to read for the store to display above the donation basket.)

Many classrooms subscribe to some of the popular children's magazines. You will have far fewer resistant readers if the latest issue and back copies of *Jack and Jill, Cricket, Ranger Rick, Sports Illustrated Kids, National Geographic Kids,* and *Zoobooks* are available for children to read during independent reading time.

Another inexpensive source of motivating reading materials are the news magazines for children, including *Scholastic News, Weekly Reader,* and *Time for Kids*. They generally cost about $4.00 per copy and you get a "desk copy" with orders of 10 to 12 copies. Teachers across a grade level often share the magazines, with each classroom receiving 2 or 3 copies. These news magazines deal with topics of real interest to kids, and reading interest is always heightened on the day that a new issue arrives.

Be sure you make the materials you read aloud to your students available for them to read. Wanting to read the book the teacher read is one of the major reasons children give for choosing particular books. And don't forget to read aloud some easy books (but call them "everyone" books) so that all your students can read on their own some of the books you read to them. Including concept and alphabet books in your teacher read-aloud and reading them aloud to the children several times will ensure that even your most struggling readers can feel successful during the independent reading time.

Talk with Your Students about Their Reading

Early in the year when you are getting your students in the habit of reading every day and gradually increasing the time for independent reading, circulate around and have whispered conversations with individual children about their books. Once the independent reading time is well established, schedule conferences with four or five students each day. Use this time to monitor each child's reading, encourage the children in their individual reading interests, and help children with book selection if needed.

To make your reading conferences something your students look forward to (instead of dreading), think of them as conversations rather than interrogations. Here are some "conference starters" you might use to set a positive and encouraging tone for reading conferences:

"Let's see, what have you got for me today?"

"Oh good, another book about ocean animals. I had no idea there were so many books about ocean animals!"

"I see you have bookmarked two pages to share with me. Read these pages to me and tell me why you chose them."

"I never knew there was so much to learn about animals in the ocean. I am so glad you bring such interesting books to share with me each week. You are turning me into an ocean animals expert!"

"I can't wait to see what you bring to share with me next week!"

One trick to make sure your conferences are "kid-centered" conversations rather than interrogations is to put the job of preparing for the conference on the child. Before you begin conferences, use modeling and role-playing to help the children learn what their job is in the conference. The children choose the book (or magazine) they want to share and bookmark the part they want to share. Make sure your students know that since you will only have three or four minutes with each student, they must prepare and be ready for the conference. After role-playing and modeling, many teachers post a chart to remind children of their responsibilities on the day of their conference.

Rather than arbitrarily assigning one-fifth of the class to the different conference days, many teachers divide up their struggling and most advanced readers across the days. The first child listed on each day is one

Getting Ready for Your Reading Conference

1. Pick the book or magazine you want to share.

2. Choose a part to read to me and practice this part.

3. Write the title and page number on a bookmark and put the bookmark in the right place.

4. Think about what you want to talk to me about. Some possibilities are:

   - What you like about this book
   - Why you chose this part to read to me
   - Other good parts of the book
   - What you think will happen (if you haven't finished the book)
   - What you are thinking about sharing with me next week
   - Who you think would also like this book

of the five most struggling readers. The second child is one of the most advanced readers.

Teachers often spend an extra minute with the struggling reader scheduled for the day. Struggling readers often need help selecting books they can read, and after the child shares the book for that day, the teacher may want to help the child select some books for the next week. Advanced readers might also need an extra minute of help with book selection. These excellent readers often read books that are too easy for them. Certainly, reading easy books is pleasurable for everyone, but it is nice for the teacher to nudge them forward in their book selection. Clever teachers do this in a "seductive" rather than a heavy-handed way:

> "Carla, I know you love mysteries, and the other day when I was in the library, I found two mysteries that made me think of you. Listen to this." (Teacher reads blurb on the back of each mystery to Carla.) "Now I have to warn you: These mysteries are a little longer and harder than the ones you usually read, but you are such a good reader, I know you could handle them if you wanted to."

Carla is probably delighted that the teacher thought of her and thinks she could read harder mysteries and will very likely "take the bait" and go off with some mysteries closer to her advanced reading level.

When students read books they *want* to read, they read more. Sharing those books once a week with someone who "oohs and aahs" about their reading choices is also a sure-fire motivator.

Conference Schedule

Day 1	Day 2	Day 3	Day 4	Day 5
Todd	Marisol	Julio	Shandra	Ian
Carla	Belinda	Tyrone	Tracy	Christine
Patrice	Carlos	Vincent	Tiffany	Mike
Tony	Antoine	Elizabeth	Richard	Sandy
Alex	Michael	Trisha	Matt	Juan

Make Time for Sharing and Talk

Children who read also enjoy talking to their classmates about what they have read. In fact, Manning and Manning (1984) found that providing time for children to interact with one another about reading material enhanced the effects of independent reading on both reading achievement and attitudes. In some classrooms, the independent reading time ends with a Reader's Chair in which one or two children each day do a book talk. They show a favorite book and read or tell a little about the book and then try to "sell" the book to the rest of the class. Their selling techniques appear to be quite effective, since these books are usually quickly seen in the hands of many of their classmates.

Another quick and simple way to encourage talk about books is to choose one day each week as a "quick share day." When the independent reading time is up, each child writes his or her name and the name of a favorite book read this week on an index card. Children then roam around the room and choose at least three other children to talk to about their chosen "great read." Children sign each other's cards to demonstrate that they have communicated about the book. When the sharing time is up, the cards are posted "collage style" somewhere in the room so that everyone can see what all their classmates have been reading that week.

In some classrooms, "reading parties" are held on one afternoon every two or three weeks. Children's names are pulled from a jar, and they form a group of three or four in which everyone gets to share their favorite book. Reading parties, like other parties, often include refreshments, such as popcorn or cookies. Children develop all kinds of tasty associations with books and sharing books.

Finding time for children to talk about books is not easy in today's crowded curriculum. There is, however, a part of each day that is not well used in most elementary classrooms—the last 15 minutes of the day. Many teachers have found that they can successfully schedule weekly reading sharing time if they utilize those last 15 minutes. Here is an example of how this sharing time works in one classroom.

Every Thursday afternoon, the teacher gets the children completely ready to be dismissed 15 minutes before the final bell rings. Notes to go home are distributed.

Book bags are packed. Chairs are placed on top of the desks. The teacher then uses index cards and writes down each child's name on a card. The index cards are shuffled, and the first five names—which will form the first group—are called. These children go to a corner of the room that will always be the meeting place for the first group. The next five names that come out will form the second group, which will go to its designated place. The process continues until all five or six groups are formed, and the children are in their places. Now each child has two minutes to read, tell, show, act out, or otherwise share something from what she or he has been reading this week. The children share in the order that their names were called. The first person called for each group is the leader. Each person has exactly two minutes and is timed by a timer. When the timer sounds, the next person gets two minutes. If a few minutes remain after all the children have had their allotted two minutes, the leader of each group selects something to share with the whole class.

Teachers who have used such a procedure to ensure that children have a chance to talk with others about what they read on a regular basis find that the children are more enthusiastic about reading. Comments such as "I'm going to stump them with these riddles when I get my two minutes" and "Wait 'til I read the scary part to everyone" are proof that sharing helps motivate reading. The popularity of the books shared with other children is further proof. Having discussions on a specified afternoon each week puts this procedure on the schedule and ensures that it will get done. Using the cards to form the groups is quick and easy and helps ensure that children will interact with many different children over the course of the year.

Make Time for Teacher Read-Aloud and Independent Reading

In today's crowded curriculum with so much emphasis on standards and tests, you may feel that you can no longer afford the luxury of taking time every day to read to your students, to develop their reading habit by engaging them in independent reading. When you consider that most new words students add to their vocabularies were probably encountered during reading, the decision to eliminate these time-tested activities seems very shortsighted. The size of your students' meaning vocabulary is the biggest determinant of comprehension. People who read more have larger vocabularies. Your students will read more if you regularly read aloud to them, provide time for independent reading, and encourage them to share their reading with you and with each other. If helping your students build large vocabularies is one of your big instructional goals, teacher read-aloud and independent reading are not luxuries—they are necessities.

chapter 3

Tell Your Students to Talk!

If there were a fly on the wall in your classroom, how many times would it hear you speaking these words?

> "It's not time to talk now!"
> "Why is there talking now?"
> "You don't need to talk while you . . ."

"You know we don't talk when . . ."
"NO talking!"

Talking is one of the biggest discipline issues most teachers face! Kids (and adults) like to talk, and being silent for long periods of time is unnatural! Imagine that the words your students are learning are tools. We use tools to accomplish tasks or to make something easier or to do it better. Words are the tools we use to communicate. The more words students have in their tool kits, the better they will be able to communicate. Talking is one of the major ways we use our words, our tools, to communicate. The new words we use as we talk become not just words whose meaning we are trying to learn, but words we own and use to communicate our ideas more clearly and precisely. This chapter will suggest a variety of ways to foster productive talk in your classroom and to turn your students' natural inclination to talk from an instructional liability to an instructional asset.

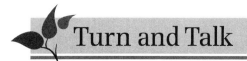

Turn and Talk

The simplest way to encourage productive talk in your classroom is to seat your students in talking partners and periodically tell them to Turn and Talk. Once you get in the habit of using talking partners, you will find numerous opportunities throughout your school day to have your students turn and talk. Think about your day and decide which turn-and-talk opportunities you could incorporate.

Turn and Talk during Read-Aloud

In the previous chapter, I suggested that you utilize Turn and Talk during your teacher read-aloud. Depending on what you are reading to them, there are numerous possibilities for productive talk. Before reading, you can encourage your students to make connections and predictions or summarize what they have already learned.

> "Today I am going to read you a book about the very first
> Thanksgiving. Look at the picture on the cover of this book and

talk to your partner about what you see and what you think is happening."

"Today I am going to read you this article from our new *Sports Illustrated Kids*. I will quickly show you each picture. Talk to your partner about what you see and what you think this article will be about."

"We have read the first four chapters of this book. Tell your partner what you remember from these chapters and what you think will happen in Chapter Five. The title of Chapter Five is 'A Surprise Visitor.'"

"Today I am going to read a biography about Abraham Lincoln. Talk to your partner about what you know about Abraham Lincoln."

Notice that all these before-reading prompts are things you probably would have asked the entire class before you had established talking partners. Only a few of your students would have had a chance to talk, however, and you might have needed to admonish some eager sharers who had spoken out without raising their hands!

Once your students are seated in talking partners, you can stop a few times in the midst of reading and re-engage them with a question:

"We have learned a lot about penguins. Look at this picture and talk to your partner about what you think we will learn on this page."

"Janine is really worried about losing the class stuffed rabbit. Do you think she will find him before Monday morning? What will the teacher say if she doesn't find him?"

When you have finished the reading for the day, you can ask your students to reflect on what you have read with some simple questions. For stories, ask them to:

"Talk with your partner about your favorite part."

For informational text, ask them to:

"Share with your partner the most interesting new facts you learned."

If you do this consistently, your students will become more active listeners during your read-aloud, knowing that they will soon get a chance to share their opinions about favorite parts or fascinating facts!

Turn and Talk for Sharing

Do you gather your students together on Monday morning and give them a chance to share something that happened over the weekend? Consider having your students share with their talking partners rather than with the whole group. They won't have to wait their turn or remember to raise their hands, and more children will be able to do more talking. Listen in on their conversations and then invite a few children to share something interesting their partner told them.

"Carl, could you tell all of us where David went this weekend?"

"Martin, can you summarize what Jason told you happened to his dog this weekend?"

"Lisa, tell everyone what Carla told you about her baby brother."

Highlighting a few events you know everyone will be interested in will keep everyone engaged in the activity. Having the partner recount what he or she heard encourages good listening—another skill most children need lots of opportunities to practice!

In addition to Monday morning sharing, there are probably many times during the day when you want students to share something. In the previous chapter, I suggested that readers like to talk about what they are reading with their friends. In addition to, or instead of, the more structured sharing opportunities suggested in Chapter 2, you can just establish a procedure of ending each independent reading time with a "two-minute" share. When you signal them, talking partners get together and talk about what they have read that day.

To pique interest in a new topic or unit, you can ask your students to tell their partners everything they already know about the topic and any experiences they have had related to that topic. After the partner sharing, you may want to list the combined class knowledge under the "Know" column of a KWL chart. Give them a minute to talk with their partners about what they would like to learn and then list their questions in the W column. Periodically, as you study the topic, let them look at what the class has listed in the "Learn" column and have them decide with their partners what new things they would like to have added to the chart.

Turn and Talk Before You Let Anyone Answer a Question

How many questions do you ask your students each day? Depending on the grade you teach, you can probably hear your voice in some of these questions:

"Who can tell me what month it is?"

"Last Thursday, we began our unit on plant life. Who remembers what we did?"

"Can anyone tell me what a quadrilateral is?"

"Before we go to lunch, let's review the lunchroom rules. Who can tell me one of them?"

"Do any of you know where the Olympics will be held this summer?"

"We are working on revising our pieces for our class book on explorers. What are some ways we can make our good writing even better?"

If some of these questions sounded familiar to you, and if you could easily add 20 or 30 more questions to this list, you are probably convinced that you ask a lot of questions every day! What happens after you ask a question? In most classrooms, some hands get raised, and some students blurt out answers when it isn't "their turn." Notice who is raising their hands and who is not and you will realize that, regardless of the question, some students always raise their hands and some students never do. The same impulsive students are the ones who blurt out the answers—in spite of your daily reminders about hand raising! Now imagine that for some of these questions you use Turn and Talk.

"Quickly tell your partner what month we are just starting."

"Last Thursday, we began our unit on plant life. Tell your partner everything you remember about what we did."

"We have been learning about shapes. Tell your partner what a quadrilateral is."

"Before we go to lunch, let's review the lunchroom rules. Talk with your partner about the rules and why they are important."

"Do any of you know where the Olympics will be held this summer? Tell your partner what you think."

"We are working on revising our pieces for our class book on explorers. Talk with your partner about some ways you can make your piece even better."

Research and common sense tell us that giving students "wait time" to think about their answers to questions increases both the quantity and quality of student answers. But waiting before you let anyone raise their hands is easier said than done—particularly when you have some chronic "blurters" in your classroom. Giving your students a very brief time to talk before anyone gives an answer encourages more students to think and participate. As you wait while they talk, you can listen in and then highlight the answers you want shared with everyone.

Turn and Talk to Help Students Summarize, Integrate, and Apply Information

For most lessons, you begin with something that helps students connect what they know to the new things they are going to learn. At the end of the lesson, you probably do something to help students summarize what they have learned and integrate or apply the new knowledge. What happens in your classroom when you pose the "closure" question?

"Who can tell me what we learned today about quadrilaterals?"

"What specific events are you looking forward to during the Olympics this summer?"

Do the same students always raise their hands while others almost never do? Do some students blurt out answers without raising their hands? Do some of the students who raise their hands not have their thoughts together or can't remember what the question was?

The most common response to the parental question "What did you learn in school today?" is "Nothing!" You can change this and help your students learn to summarize, integrate, and apply what they are learning if you regularly ask your students to:

> "Pretend your partner is your mom or dad asking, 'What did you learn in school today?' Tell them what you learned about quadrilaterals during math."

> "Pretend your partner is your mom or dad and tell them which particular events you are looking forward to during the Olympics this summer."

Think-Pair-Share

Think-Pair-Share is a variation of Turn and Talk in which students are asked to think quietly for one minute before they pair up with their partners. After one minute of thinking time, they pair with their assigned partner and talk, just as in Turn and Talk. The sharing that follows can be with the whole class, or pairs can be combined into quartets in which each child shares with the group what the other partner has said. Needing to share what your partner said promotes good listening, a skill all your students probably need to work on. Think-Pair-Share can be used to have students talk about all the situations described as possibilities for Turn and Talk.

Seize the Small Opportunities for Productive Talk!

Did you notice that the talking partner suggestions are not adding "one more thing" you have to fit into your already busy day? Good instruction at any grade level in any subject involves having students talk, share, respond to questions, and integrate new knowledge and ideas. In most classrooms, however, a few students do all the talking, and many other students are not listening! Incorporating quick partner-talk opportunities throughout your day can dramatically increase the quantity and quality of talking and listening for all of your students. To talk and listen, they have to use their communication tools—words!

Turn and Talk and Think-Pair-Share—Good for Everyone But Essential for English Language Learners

Do you remember how you learned a new language? In addition to reading and practice exercises, did your teachers provide opportunities for you to speak the language? When you did speak the language, were you required to talk to the whole class? How did you feel about speaking to the class in the new language? When learning a new language, receptive vocabulary—words you can understand when you read them or hear them—develops way ahead of expressive vocabulary—words you can use to express yourself as you speak or write. Lots of small turn-and-talk or think-pair-share opportunities throughout the day provide safe places for your English language learners to try out their speaking skills. Assign them an empathetic, supportive partner (perhaps a budding teacher?) and watch them use their word tools to communicate in the new language.

Structured Discussions

Turn and Talk and Think-Pair-Share are routines that will promote the learning of new words as they are needed to accomplish the task set for the talking partners. Most of the time, we do not specify which words partners should use as they are talking. We do need, however, to have students talk using the new words we have chosen to teach them. To accomplish this, put your students into groups of three or four (call them *trios* or *quartets* to add those two words to their toolboxes!) and give them a specific task to accomplish with a specified group of words. To accomplish the task, students have to talk. Here are some adaptable ways to structure discussions and have your students use targeted words.

List, Group, and Label

List, Group, and Label is a lesson format that was developed in the sixties by Hilda Taba (1967), an expert in concept development in social studies. It can be used at all grade levels and in all subject areas to help students develop

awkward	tradition	venture	adamant	burrow	adventurous
plentiful	reveal	ancestor	survivor	obstacles	capable
mystical	scarce	contented	shallow	badger	stagger
hardship	crafty	peculiar	destructive	descendant	pointless
captivity	outstanding	inflexible	fragile	abundant	heroic

depth of word meanings. List, Group, and Label lessons occur after the students have encountered the words in some context and have had some previous experiences with those words. Now you want them to extend their experiences with those words, and you want them to use these word tools to communicate through talking. Above is a list of words one fourth-grade class had encountered and discussed when reading in their literature circles.

The children met in their assigned quartets and were given a sheet with these words on them. The teacher and students read the words and gave a brief meaning for each, referring to the story context to remind everyone of the meaning of the word in that context.

Next the students cut the sheet along the lines and laid the 30 words out in front of them. Their task was to choose some words that went together in some way. Once they chose the words, their task was to come up with a label for them. A recorder wrote down the first group they made and the label for the group:

Positive Character Traits

adventurous
crafty
heroic
outstanding
capable

Quickly, they put these words back in with the others and formed another group:

Negative Character Traits

fragile
inflexible
destructive
peculiar
awkward

They formed two more groups before the 15-minute time limit was up:

Relatives	Difficulties
ancestor	hardship
descendant	obstacles
	captivity

The teacher gathered the students together, and each quartet got to choose one of their groups to share with the class. They read the words in the group, but did not tell the label. They then called on volunteers to guess what label they had given the group. The quartet then shared the label they had come up with. Another quartet shared one of their groups, called on volunteers to guess the label, and revealed the label they had come up with.

This example lesson used words collected during reading lessons. Applications of this lesson template in math, social studies, and art can be found in the subject-area chapters devoted to those subjects. List, Group, and Label is an example of a structured discussion in which your goal is to have students talk about words they have already met and had some experience with in hopes that they will now "own" the words.

These Words Go Together Because . . .

These Words Go Together Because . . . is similar to List, Group, and Label in that students work in small groups to decide how words from a list are connected. In a third-grade class, the teacher took the 24 words that had been taught during Three Read-Aloud Words lessons (described in Chapter 5). He gave students a sheet that contained the 24 words and four These Words Go Together Because . . . sentence frames.

loyal	opponent	Australia	victorious	ancient	brilliant
coward	explorer	fierce	journey	predator	continent
responsible	solution	courageous	capture	distant	persevere
frigid	clever	Antarctica	undefeated	perilous	prey

1. _____ and _____ go together
   because _____.

2. _____ and _____ go together
   because _____.

3. _____ and _____ go together
   because _____.

4. _____ and _____ go together
   because _____.

Trios worked together for 10 minutes and completed four sentences. When the time was up, the class gathered. Each trio read one of their sentences, stopping after the word *because* and calling on classmates to guess why they had put those two words together. Here are some of their sentences. The part following *because* is intentionally written without spaces between words so that you can try guessing their reason, like their classmates did.

> Loyal and responsible go together because
> ifyouareloyalyouarebeingresponsibletoyourfriend.
>
> Coward and explorer go together because
> youcouldn'tbeanexplorerifyouwereacoward.
>
> Australia and Antarctica go together because theyarebothcontinents.
>
> Antarctica and frigid go together because itisveryveryfrigidinAntarctica.
>
> Journey and explorer go together because explorersgoonlongjourneys.
>
> Brilliant and clever go together because theybothmeanyouareverysmart.

If you had fun guessing the reasons, you see the "hook" in this activity, which gets kids eagerly completing the sentences and saying the words. If you are thinking of some other sentences your students could write, you see how These Words Go Together Because . . . would generate a lot of productive talk.

Fill in My Blank

In this activity, students work together in trios or quartets to write sentences containing one of the vocabulary words. When they write a sentence, they underline the vocabulary word. They write as many sentences as they can in 10 minutes. When the class gathers, each group reads one of its sentences, saying "blank" for the underlined word. The rest of the class writes the word they think goes in the blank. The goal is to write such a good sentence that almost everyone guesses correctly what goes in the blank. Here are some sentences students created based on the same word list used in These Words Go Together Because . . . Can you guess which word goes in the blank?

Australia is a _____.

Our team won every game and was _____ for the season.

A person who is 100 years old is very _____.

Christopher Columbus was a famous _____.

If the temperature is below 0°, it is very _____.

Guess What Word I Am

This time, students are given a list of words, and they decide on a word to act out. They plan a short skit and then do this skit for their classmates, who have to guess which word is being acted out. You may be a bit skeptical about this activity, but give it a try. Kids are less self-conscious than adults and come up with clever ways of demonstrating the words. Even if the classmates don't guess the word, coming up with the skit requires a lot of talk about the word!

A–Z Charts

For this activity, students come up with the list of words. Teachers often use this activity at the end of a unit to review important concepts. Students work in quartets or trios to list words related to the topic. The goal is to see how many words they can list and to have at least one word in each box. Give students a chart with 24 boxes (x, y, and z in one box). They brainstorm words in their small groups for 15 minutes, and then the class comes together and shares their words. Classmates can challenge a word if the connection is not clear, and the group that included the word has to explain their thinking. Here is the A–Z Chart one group of fifth-graders came up with. Are there any words you would like to challenge? This group could not think of a word beginning with Q. Can you think of one?

A	B	C	D	E	F
assassinated Atlanta Alabama Andrew	birthday bus boycott	civil	D.C. dream discrimination	equality	freedom fair

G	H	I	J	K	L
guards	holiday honor	integration integrity	January junior	King	Luther loyal

M	N	O	P	Q	R
Montgomery march Monday minister Memphis	negro Nobel nonviolent	opportunity organize orator	peace prize protest poverty		racism rights rally

S	T	U	V	W	XYZ
segregation service stamp SCLC speech	Tennessee target	unfair unjust unified	values valor Viet Nam	Washington	Young zealot

Numbered Heads Together

Numbered Heads Together, described by Kagan (1994), is a way of organizing a discussion and holding all the group members responsible for the thinking the group does. To organize the groups, you have the children count off so that there is a one, two, three, and four in each group. When the groups are formed, the teacher gives them a question to discuss:

"What are some examples of physical and chemical changes we see every day?"

"What adaptations do animals make to survive in their habitats?"

"How does technology make our lives different from the lives of our grandparents?"

When the students have had a few minutes to discuss the question, the teacher draws a card to determine which group member is going to share the group's answer with the whole class. If the teacher draws the number three, all the children who were number three in their group stand up and share their group's answer.

Numbered Heads Together is an excellent way to engage all children in thinking and talking about a topic. No one (including the teacher) knows who will share the group's thinking, so everyone has a stake in participating in the discussion. If you have worried that some members of a group do all the work when your students meet in small groups, try Numbered Heads Together and watch the motivation, engagement, and confidence of all your students grow.

Jigsaw Groups

Another cooperative group discussion format promoted by Kagan (1994) puts students into small groups in which every member is responsible for learning their group's content. Imagine for example that your class is learning about the different classes of animals. You assign your students to one of six groups—mammals, reptiles, birds, amphibians, insects, and fish. You have 25 students, so you assign four students to each group and let the extra student choose a group to join. The class has been studying these different classes of animals, and each group is responsible for listing some characteristics of their class and coming up with examples.

While they are talking and coming up with the characteristics and examples, you go around and give each child a small red, blue, green, or yellow sticker. When they have had sufficient time to complete their discussion, the students reassemble themselves in the four corners of the room, which you have designated as red, blue, green, or yellow. The new groups have six members, each of which has one piece of the puzzle (thus the name—Jigsaw Groups). (The extra child goes with the other person from his group with the same color, and they both share their information.) Going in alphabetical order by the name of the animal class they represent, each person in the new group shares the characteristics and examples of amphibians, birds, fish, insects, mammals, and reptiles.

English Language Learners in Discussions

Like Turn and Talk, structured discussions, Numbered Heads Together, and Jigsaw Groups provide a safe environment in which your English language learners can talk and increase their depth of knowledge about words the class is working on. Carefully consider whom you place in the groups with your students who are learning English. If you have another student who speaks the same language but whose English is more developed, include that child, along with one or two other students who will be supportive and help your English language learners develop the confidence that they can communicate in English. If you have a student whose English is very limited, make that student the extra student in the group so that he or she shares responsibility for sharing information with others.

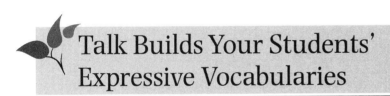

Talk Builds Your Students' Expressive Vocabularies

Many students see new vocabulary words as words they have to study and learn, rather than as tools that help them communicate. Talk is the most basic form of communication. Kids—like adults—love to talk! The trick in the classroom is to make that talk productive. Language Standard Three of the Common Core State Standards requires that students learn how to participate in discussions.* Third-graders are expected to:

> Engage effectively in a range of collaborative discussions (one-on-one, in groups, and teacher-led) with diverse partners on grade 3 topics and texts, building on others' ideas and expressing their own clearly.

© Copyright 2010. National Governors Association Center for Best Practices and Council of Chief State School Officers. All rights reserved.

This chapter has suggested a variety of ways that you can infuse productive talk into all areas of the curriculum throughout the school day. When you incorporate partner and small-group talk about topics you are studying, your students will learn the academic vocabulary they need to communicate what they are learning. They will also learn how to participate in discussions, learning from the ideas of others, and how to clearly express their ideas.

chapter 4

Writing Builds Expressive Vocabulary

Given the choice, would you rather write or talk? In the previous chapter, I suggested that kids love to talk and that you can capitalize on this human affinity for talking to help your students

add words to their vocabulary toolboxes. Unfortunately, the attitude of most kids toward writing is not so positive. Unlike talking, writing does not come naturally. You have to learn to write—and you have to juggle many balls at the same time. As you write, you have to decide:

- What you want to communicate.
- What form the writing is going to take.
- What words will most precisely and vividly communicate your ideas.

In addition to these major writing decisions, you have to juggle the small—but important—details.

- Is this the end of my sentence? What punctuation should I put if it is?
- I should include dialogue to show what my character is like, but I can never remember where the quotation marks and commas go.
- Is this a new paragraph? I haven't indented in awhile.
- "The package was enormous," but I can't spell *enormous,* so I will just write "very big."
- I know you capitalize proper nouns, but is *summer* a proper noun?

Writing helps students learn to use their new word tools to communicate more clearly, vividly, and precisely. Because writing is so complex and many students view writing as a chore, your efforts to get them to develop ownership of new words through writing will be most productive if you infuse small doses of "quick-writes" throughout your day. Which of these quick-writes will help your students build their expressive vocabularies, and where would they fit into your day?

Think-Write-Pair-Share

Think-Write-Pair-Share just adds a writing step to the Think-Pair-Share activity suggested in the chapter on talking. Instead of giving students one minute to think, you give them two minutes to write down what they are going to share. The types of questions you pose can be the same types of questions described for partner talk in Chapter 3. You can also ask some questions designed specifically to elicit known or new vocabulary.

- In two minutes, you and your partner are going to talk about reptiles. Grab a scrap of paper and write down what you know about reptiles.
- We are going to go on a virtual fieldtrip to Plymouth where the first Thanksgiving took place. Write down what you know about the first Thanksgiving that you can share with your partner.
- I just flipped the lights on and off. The lights work because of electricity. Write down what you know about how electricity gets into our classroom and why we need it.
- We are going to start studying percents in math today. Write down some percents you see in the world and where you see them.

"Begin with what your students know" is a time-honored principle of teaching. Learning occurs when new knowledge is connected to previous knowledge. The knowledge you have about any topic is represented by the words you can relate to that topic. As students write and then share their knowledge about a topic, they access the vocabulary tools they currently possess and create slots in their brains to which they can add new vocabulary tools.

Fast-forward now to an hour or a week later when you have been building knowledge about animals, Thanksgiving, electricity, or percentages. Now you want your students to integrate their new knowledge—and vocabulary—with their old knowledge and vocabulary. Once again, you can give them two minutes to think and write before they talk with their partners.

- I know you have all learned a lot about reptiles. In two minutes, I will let you talk with your partner about what you learned. Grab a scrap of paper and write down what you learned about reptiles.
- Did you enjoy our virtual fieldtrip to Plymouth? Write down what you learned about the first Thanksgiving that you can share with your partner.

- Write down what you now know about how electricity gets into our classroom and why we need it.

- We see percents everywhere. Write down some percents and where you see them and prepare to tell your partner why learning about percents is important.

Think-Pair-Write-Share quick-writes have to be quick, and they won't work if everyone has to find a piece of paper and sharpen a pencil. The teacher in this classroom recycles paper that is only printed on one side by tearing it into "scraps" which sit in baskets at each table grouping. Special pens (which must go back into the baskets and are never allowed in desks) make pencil sharpening unnecessary and are more fun to write with! It is also important to specify and stick to the time limit. Two minutes is plenty of time for students to recall and jot down most of what they know. Students who don't know much don't get too squirmy in two minutes, and students who know a lot enjoy racing to write down an impressive array of facts before the time is up.

Two-in-One True Sentences

Have you ever asked your students to write sentences with vocabulary words and gotten some sentences like these?

The boy was <u>loyal</u>.
I like <u>mammals</u>.
He was a <u>president</u>.

Putting words in sentences does nothing to help students add words to their vocabularies if they figure out how to create meaningless sentences that use the word correctly but indicate nothing about its meaning.

One year, while teaching fourth grade, I told my students they had to make good sentences with the words. When asked what a good sentence was, I declared that the sentence told something about the meaning of the word. Now I got sentences like this:

Loyal means faithful.
Mammals are animals.
A president means a leader of a nation.

These were a little better, but it was clear the students were just using the dictionary definition to create a sentence. They still weren't building their meanings. (My suspicions were confirmed when I asked the author of the "Loyal means faithful" sentence what *faithful* meant and she responded immediately, "Loyal!"

Two-in-One True Sentences require students to use at least two of the vocabulary words to write one true sentence. Imagine that your students have been learning about government and elections and they have this bank of vocabulary words:

president	senator	representative	election	Supreme Court
executive	Congress	Democrat	Republican	justice
legislative	judicial	government	democracy	candidate
national	campaign	minority	majority	party

They have five minutes to write three Two-in-One Sentences. Each sentence must use two of the vocabulary words, but they can use more words as long as the sentence makes sense. Here are some sentences written by fourth-graders. They were told to underline each vocabulary word and to change the form of the word to fit the sentence (*election, elect, elected*).

The president is the head of the government.

The justices are in the Supreme Court.

The Congress is the legislative part of government.

The Republican Party won the most votes, so they were the majority in Congress.

The senators and the representatives are all in the Congress.

Eureka! Good sentences that are not copied from the dictionary and tell something about the word! Notice that several sentences use more than two words, and one sentence actually uses five! When you tell your students they need to use at least two words, some of your clever (and competitive students) take on the challenge of using more than two. While sharing their sentences, the boy who wrote the sentence about the Republican Party read his and then proudly announced, "I used five!" From then on, in this classroom, the game was on. Students no longer were happy with using two of the words; they wanted to see how many they could get in and still have a true sentence.

Journals

In many classrooms, children keep content journals in which they record ideas, examples, predictions, summaries, vocabulary, and other specifics of what they are learning and thinking about. Depending on your goals and curriculum, you may want your students to keep a science, math, or social studies journal. Give everyone a notebook reserved for that purpose or staple together some paper and let students create a cover. Encourage students to include sketches and drawings as well as writing in their journals so that your students who are more visual than verbal will have opportunities to record their thoughts. You will find specific suggestions for building vocabulary using math and science journals in Chapters 8 and 9.

Cinquains

Cinquains, five-line poems that describe something, are quick and fun to write and excellent vehicles for developing vocabulary. There are various forms for the different lines, but to develop vocabulary, I like the form in which the second line has two describing words or a phrase, the third line has three examples or three "ing" verbs, and the fourth line has a four-word phrase. The teacher and the class brainstorm words for each line, and then students choose words from their list or make their own choices to create their cinquain. Here is the word bank brainstormed by one class as they were culminating a math unit on quadrilaterals.

Topic	Words for Line 2	Examples for Line 3	Four-Word Phrases
Quadrilaterals	Straight lines Four sides Closed Shape	Square Rectangle Rhombus Trapezoid Kite Parallelogram	Always has four sides Polygons have four sides Some have parallel sides All have four angles Squares have right angles Angles = 360 degrees Squares have equal sides

Here are two of the cinquains they wrote. One student chose from the brainstormed list. The other student utilized his creativity. Both students used writing to think about quadrilaterals and build math vocabulary.

Quadrilaterals

Four sides

Kites, Squares, Rectangles

All have four angles

Quadrilaterals

Quadrilaterals

Neat shapes

Rectangles, Squares, Rhombuses

All have parallel lines

Parallelograms

A Ticket Out the Door

In many classrooms, teachers ask students to do a quick-write as their ticket out of class. Students think about what they learned and respond to prompts such as:

Today in math I learned how to . . .   This is how I do it . . .

Today in science we experimented with . . .   I learned that . . .

Today we read about . . .   Three interesting things I learned were . . .

Some days you might want students to compare something they learned to something they already knew.

I already knew that . . .   But today I learned that . . .
I used to think that . . .   But now I think . . .

In addition to thinking about what they are learning, your students also need to think about what else they would like to learn.

One question I have about . . .   is . . .
What thing I am interested in and want to learn more about is . . .

It is important for students to think about what they are learning and assess their own understanding and attitudes, so on some days, ask them to respond to an "easiest/hardest," an "I liked/didn't like," or an "I'm confused about" prompt.

In today's class, it was easy for me to . . .   But it was hard for me to . . .

What I liked best about today's lesson was . . .   What I didn't like was . . .

One thing I am still confused about is . . .

Students need to learn that their effort and engagement matter in how much they learn, so you may want to include some prompts to help them assess this.

Today I tried really hard to . . .
Today my effort level was . . .   because . . .

Teachers who regularly give students two minutes at the end of class to reflect upon their learning report that student engagement increases and students become more aware of and take more control of their own learning. Another advantage of these exit-ticket quick-writes is that you can quickly assess how well your students are grasping the main points of the lesson and see what you need to reteach or can build on for the next lesson.

Friday Homework—Top Three Things I Learned This Week

In many classrooms, homework is not assigned on Fridays. There is one homework assignment, however, which is popular with both students and parents. On Friday afternoons, just before dismissal, give students a few minutes to write a letter to their parents or other caregivers. The letter should not be long, but it should include a few things the student found most interesting this week. Since a week is a long time, you may want to have your class brainstorm some possibilities and create a class Top Ten list. Students can pick from this list or add their own favorite things. If you incorporate the Top Three Things Letter into your weekly routine, you will be sure to have at least one opportunity each week for students to think about what they are learning. As your students talk with parents and other caregivers about what they have learned, you have created a weekly opportunity for your students to talk. As they write and talk, they will be using and building their vocabulary and language tools.

Dear _____,

I learned a lot at school this week. Here are the top three things I learned.

1. _____

_____

2. _____

_____

3. _____

_____

Please sign to show that we talked about what I learned.

Signature _____

Quick-Writes for English Language Learners

What do you remember about your experience learning another language? Were you better at reading the language than you were at listening to it or speaking it? How did you feel when you were asked to write something in the new language? For most learners, writing is the hardest communication piece. Think about the things that make writing hard in your first language—choosing what to say, precise vocabulary, spelling, and mechanics—and multiply this complexity in a language that you are in the process of learning. Using their new English vocabulary to express themselves in writing is important for your English language learners, but writing is especially difficult for them. Quick-writes are a painless way of supporting your fledgling English learners as they learn to communicate in their new language.

Infuse Quick-Writes Throughout Your School Day

Think of something that is difficult for you, perhaps learning how to use a new technology or exercising. When you need to do something that is difficult for you, do you try to reduce the stress by doing it in small doses and spreading those throughout the week? Learning to write clearly with vivid and precise words is a major goal for all our students. But writing, unlike talking, is not something most of us find easy and natural. Quick-writes are just that—quick—and unlike the other kinds of writing students do, is not revised, edited, or published. Teachers are not expected to grade them or create a rubric to evaluate them. Quick-writes can help your students learn the content you are trying to teach them and develop the vocabulary tools to communicate what they are learning.

chapter 5

Teaching Vocabulary Independence

"Give me a fish, and I eat for a day. Teach me to fish, and I eat for a lifetime."

The ultimate goal of instruction is that students become independent and generative, using the strategies and knowledge they have gained to "learn for a lifetime." In Chapter 1, you learned that most new word meanings students acquire as they progress through school are learned independently as they read. Increasing the amount of reading that students do and building their intrinsic motivation to choose to read is essential for vocabulary development. In fact, increasing the volume of reading your students do is so important to the long-term goal of vocabulary growth that Chapter 2 of this book was dedicated to helping you revisit and recommit to the time-honored practices of teacher read-aloud and independent reading time as daily events in all elementary classrooms.

Getting your students to read more is essential for vocabulary growth, but there won't be much vocabulary growth if your students are not actively trying to figure out the meanings of unfamiliar words. What if some of your students have developed the "skip it" habit? They come to a word they don't immediately recognize or understand and, instead of using the clues available to them, they just "skip it" and keep reading. To maximize the number of words students learn from their reading, we must teach them how to use context and pictures, we must teach them word parts, and we must teach them how to combine them with context and pictures to infer meanings for new words. This chapter will provide some activities and lesson frameworks you can use to help your students break the "skip it" habit and become independent learners of new words.

Use Word Parts to Figure Out New Word Meanings

Read this fictionalized account of a high school baseball game and think about why certain words are shaded and other words have a part bolded at the beginning or end of the word.

Underdogs Win Champion**ship**

Yesterday, Smithtown made the district playoffs by winning both games of a doubleheader against Parkwood. In the first game,

Smithtown coach Jose Martinez started his best pitcher, Ivey Hanes. Hanes used his fastball and slider to shutout the Parkwood hitters for the first five innings. Meanwhile, the Bobcats' hitters scored three runs off the Grasshoppers' starter, Jock Jackson. In the first inning, Jackson's screwball and changeup looked **un**hitt**able** until Smithtown's catch**er**, Chi Park, hit an **in**cred**ible** home run over the scoreboard. In the fourth inning, Jackson got two quick outs but then could not find the strike zone. He loaded the bases with Bobcat runn**ers** and walked the next batt**er** in for an **un**earned run. Hanes batted in the Bobcats' third run with a sacrifice fly to a Parkwood outfielder that brought Eric Price home from third base. After that, Jackson **re**covered his concentration and **over**powered the next batt**er**. Jackson pitched hit**less** baseball after the fourth inning, but the damage was done. After the first game, Parkwood's coach, David Tyson, commented, "A shutout for our team was completely **un**expected. Even our best slugg**ers** struck out or hit ground**ers**. There was nothing I could do in our dugout but watch and weep!"

In the nightcap, Parkwood's starting pitch**er** was Juan Ortiz, fam**ous** for his power**ful** speedball. Smithtown countered with "Lucky" Brown, their freshman sensation, the young**est** starting pitch**er** in Bobcat history. Brown allowed the Grasshopper shortstop, Mike Williamson, to reach base on a single. Parkwood's third baseman, Ryan Ford, hit a triple to score Williamson. During Brown's windup to the next batt**er**, Ford stole home, making the score 2–0. In the fifth inning, the fireworks started with the play of the day. Bobcat infielder, Eric Price, hit a rainmaker off Ortiz. All three Grasshopper outfielders ran to catch the ball. The centerfielder, Keyshawn Upshaw, was clos**est** to it when the ball seemed to **dis**appear in the lights. After a few seconds of confus**ion**, Upshaw located the ball in the air and leaped toward it, colliding with John Rice,

Greenville's right field**er,** who had also run to the warning track. The ball barely cleared the outfield fence. Price scored his second run of the day on the home run, making the score 2–1. Then, the Bobcat catch**er,** Chi Park, hit a double off Ortiz. Coach Martinez sent in a pinch hitt**er** for his next batt**er.** Mark West, who had been a benchwarmer for the Bobcats all season, came through with a single that scored Park from second, making the score 2–2. West stole second base and then was driven home by Manuel Ho's long single, making the score 3–2 and giving Smithtown their first regular season champion**ship** in 22 years! After the game, Martinez said, "This just proves that an **under**dog like Smithtown can become the champion, if we play hard and don't give up."

What did you conclude about the shaded words? You probably noticed that all the shaded words are compound words made up of two root words. The meaning of the compound word combines the meanings of the two root words. Often the meaning of the compound word is quite obvious, even to the youngest reader. **Ballpark, outfield,** and **scoreboard** are examples of compound words with transparent meanings.

Now think about the words that have some bolded letters at the beginning: **un**hitt**able, un**earned, **un**expected, **in**credible, **dis**appear, **re**covered, **over**powered, and **under**dog. These words all have root words with another word part, prefixes added to the beginning of the word. As with compound words, sometimes the meaning of the prefixed word is transparent if you know the meaning of the root word and the prefix. The most common prefix, **un,** appears three times in this article. In all three words—**un**hittable, **un**earned, and **un**expected—**un** turns the root word into the opposite. The next three most common prefixes—**re, in,** and **dis**—are found in the words **re**covered, **in**credible, and **dis**appeared. Also, **under** and **over** are common prefixes and occur here in the words **under**dog and **over**powered.

This article also includes many words with suffixes. **Er,** meaning a person who does the action, is a common suffix that occurs in many words, including pitch**er,** catch**er,** batt**er,** hitt**er,** start**er,** runn**er**s, slugg**er**s, benchwarm**er,** infield**er,** outfield**er,** and centerfield**er.** The suffix **er** can also refer to a thing that does something, shown here by the words slid**er** and ground**er**. **Est,** meaning "most," is another common suffix and is represented here by young**est** and clos**est**. **Less** and **ful** are two other suffixes that change the meaning of words. This article contains the words hit**less** and power**ful**. Some suffixes don't change the meaning of a word but do change its grammatical function. **Able, ible, ous, sion,** and **ship** are examples of grammatical suffixes and occur in the words unhitt**able,** incred**ible,** fam**ous,** confu**sion,** and champion**ship.**

There is another very common type of suffix called an inflectional suffix and this suffix does not change meaning or grammatical function. **S, ed,** and **ing** are inflectional suffixes and occur in numerous words in everything we read, including champion**s,** leap**ed,** and collid**ing**.

In English, many of the big new words students encounter are actually smaller words combined to make compound words or smaller words with prefixes or suffixes attached to the beginning or end of the word. If students pay attention to the familiar parts of big words and if they know the meanings of common prefixes and suffixes, they can figure out the meanings of many unfamiliar words. Teaching your students to recognize and use word parts to figure out the meanings of new words is so important that the next chapter of this book contains lessons and activities you can use to help all your students capitalize on the "magic of morphology."

Use Context to Figure Out New Word Meanings

Morphology clues are contained within a single word. Context is the other words that surround an unfamiliar word. These other words often contain clues to the meaning of an unfamiliar word. Read these sentences and see whether you can use the context to figure out the meaning of the blackened word.

- A person who lives to be 100 is called a ██████████.

- My dad is an ████████████, a doctor who specializes in vision problems.

- My grandma is █████████, the most talkative person you would ever meet!

- The volcano that had been ▮▮▮▮▮▮ for 52 years became active last year and is still erupting.

- Many species of ▮▮▮▮▮▮ including frogs, toads and salamanders, are endangered or extinct.

- In the last century, many infectious diseases including polio, measles, and malaria have been drastically reduced. Only smallpox, however, has been completely ▮▮▮▮▮ worldwide.

- The United States is a nation of ▮▮▮▮▮, including many famous sports figures. At the age of 19, Martina Navratilova defected to the U.S. from Czechoslovakia. Sammy Sosa was born in the Dominican Republic. Mario Andretti began racing in Italy before coming to the United States. Patrick Ewing was 11 years old when his family came to the United States.

It doesn't matter whether you guessed the exact words, but do you see how the context, the other words in the sentence and surrounding sentences build meanings for the words, *centenarian, ophthalmologist, loquacious, dormant, amphibians, eradicated,* and *immigrants.*

These examples represent the most common type of context clues. Sometimes the context contains a definition:

- A person who lives to be 100 is called a **centenarian**.

That definition might be separated from the word by a comma:

- My dad is an **ophthalmologist,** a doctor who specializes in vision problems.

Sometimes context clues appear as synonyms:

- My grandma is **loquacious,** the most talkative person you would ever meet!

An antonym, or opposite, is another type of common context clue:

- The volcano that had been **dormant** for 52 years became active last year and is still erupting.

Clues to meaning are often contained in examples:

- Many species of **amphibians,** including frogs, toads, and salamanders, are endangered or extinct.

Finally some clues are contained in the other words in the surrounding sentences.

- In the last century many infectious diseases including polio, measles, and malaria have been drastically reduced. Only smallpox, however, has been completely **eradicated** worldwide.
- The United States is a nation of **immigrants,** including many famous sports figures. At the age of 19, Martina Navratilova defected to the U.S. from Czechoslovakia. Sammy Sosa was born in the Dominican Republic. Mario Andretti began racing in Italy before coming to the United States. Patrick Ewing was 11 years old when his family came to the United States.

In addition to providing clues to the meaning of an unfamiliar word, context can indicate which meaning of a word you should be using to understand what you are reading. If I ask you to tell me what *field* means, you might respond with answers such as:

- A place to walk through, play games on, or plant crops
- A career, like business or teaching
- To catch a baseball

Without any context, you don't know which meaning of the multimeaning word *field* to access. Now imagine that you read the word *field* in the following sentences. Notice that you automatically access the appropriate meaning.

- Every year, thousands of new jobs are created in the field of medicine.
- Wheat was planted in the north field and corn in the south field.
- Dolly Parton made it big in the country music field.
- After the victory, the fans flooded out onto the field.
- The shortstop fielded the grounder and threw it to first base.

Because context gives you clues to the meaning of new words and lets you know which meaning of a multimeaning word is correct, utilizing the context to understand what you read is essential to reading comprehension.

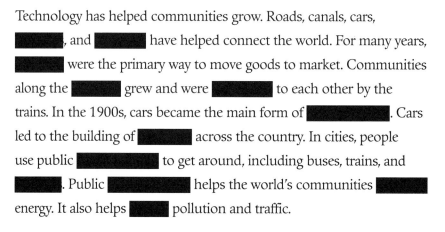

Context and Morphology—A Powerful Combination

Read this paragraph and try to guess the meanings of the words that are blacked out.

> Technology has helped communities grow. Roads, canals, cars,
> ████, and ██████ have helped connect the world. For many years,
> ██████ were the primary way to move goods to market. Communities
> along the ██████ grew and were ████████ to each other by the
> trains. In the 1900s, cars became the main form of ████████████. Cars
> led to the building of ████████ across the country. In cities, people
> use public ████████████ to get around, including buses, trains, and
> ████████. Public ████████████ helps the world's communities ████████
> energy. It also helps █████ pollution and traffic.

Now read it again and see how some familiar word parts help.

> Technology has helped communities grow. Roads, canals, cars,
> rail████, and air██████ have helped connect the world. For many years,
> rail████ were the primary way to move goods to market. Communities
> along the rail████ grew and were con██████ to each other by the
> trains. In the 1900s, cars became the main form of trans████████. Cars
> led to the building of high████ across the country. In cities, people
> use public trans████████ to get around, including buses, trains, and
> sub████. Public trans████████ helps the world's communities con██████
> energy. It also helps re█████ pollution and traffic.

Using the context along with morphology, did you figure out that the blackened words were *railroads, airplanes, connected, transportation, highways, subways, conserve,* and *reduce*?

In the article about the baseball game, you could use morphology and context to figure out some of the words. Why would a player be called a **benchwarmer**? Why would a certain kind of hit be called a **rainmaker**? Consider the context that surrounds these two words.

> Coach Martinez sent in a pinch hitter for his next batter. Mark West, who had been a benchwarmer for the Bobcats all season, came through with a single that scored Park from second, making the score 2–2.

From the context, you figure out that the **benchwarmer** is one of the Bobcat players. Because he is a pinch hitter, you know he is not a regular starter. But why is he called a **benchwarmer**? Putting together the meanings of the two roots—**bench** and **warm**—and adding **er** (the person who does the action), you figure out that he must sit on the bench a lot during games, and you realize that **benchwarmer** is a clever way of describing a player who doesn't play much and thus "warms the bench!"

> Bobcat infielder, Eric Price, hit a rainmaker off Ortiz. All three Grasshopper outfielders ran to catch the ball. The centerfielder, Keyshawn Upshaw, was closest to it when the ball seemed to disappear in the lights. After a few seconds of confusion, Upshaw located the ball in the air and leaped toward it, colliding with John Rice, Greenville's right fielder, who had also run to the warning track. The ball barely cleared the outfield fence.

From this context you realize that a **rainmaker** must be a very high ball, one so high that it could "make it rain!"

Pictures—One More Clue to Meaning

In addition to word parts and context, many unfamiliar words can be figured out by considering the clues provided by the pictures. Imagine that you are reading a magazine and you see a picture of an animal you don't immediately recognize. The animal is clearly a mammal and looks a little like a pig, but it has a stubby tail, a long pointed snout, and hoofs. "What is that animal?" you ask yourself as you start to read. The article describes some endangered animals, including the tapir you are looking at. You also read that the snout of the tapir is called a "proboscis" and that the tapir has hoofed, "splayed" toes. Wondering what splayed means, you inspect the toes in the photo and notice that they are spread quite far apart. When you finish reading the article, you have added three new words, *tapir, proboscis,* and *splayed,* to your vocabulary store, and you have a picture in your mind of what these new words mean.

Using Pictures, Context, and Word Parts to Sleuth Out the Meanings of New Words

I hope you are now convinced that it is crucial for your students not to just skip over new words when they are reading on their own but to use the clues available to them to figure out what the words mean. In this section, I will describe four lesson frameworks you can use with your students to teach them how to figure out new word meanings and to help them break the "skip it" habit.

Preview-Predict-Confirm (PPC)

When you begin to read a magazine article that has lots of pictures, do you look at the pictures before you start reading the words? In addition to piquing your interest in the topic, the pictures help you connect your prior knowledge about the topic and access appropriate word meanings. In the article referred to earlier from which you learned the new words *tapir, proboscis,* and *splayed,* there were other pictures of endangered animals that you could name and knew a lot about. Looking at pictures to start making connections, access appropriate vocabulary, and begin building new word meanings is a strategy all good readers use. Preview-Predict-Confirm (Yopp & Yopp, 2004) is a lesson framework that will teach all your students to make maximum use of the visuals in a text. Here are the steps to follow when teaching a PPC lesson.

1. Seat students in trios.
   To begin your PPC lesson, put your students in groups of three, including an advanced, average, and struggling student in each group.

2. Show students 10–15 pictures from the text and have them talk about each picture.

   Display pictures from the informational book or magazine article they are about to read, allowing trios 20 seconds to talk with each other as they look at each image. If possible, scan these pictures into a presentation and project them one at a time. Alternatively, you can gather your students close to you and show them pictures from the actual text, making sure to cover all words on the pages so that only the pictures are visible to the students.

3. Have students write words they think will occur in the text.

   When they have viewed and talked about all the images, give trios 10 minutes to write words they think will occur in the text they are about to read. Send the trios to far corners of the room to do this and ask them to use their "secret" voices so that other groups cannot hear the words they are guessing. Appoint a recorder in each group to write the words on a sheet with 27 boxes and the topic word in the center.

	Penguins	

4. Have trios pick a common word, a unique word, and a most interesting word.

   When the 10 minutes they are allotted to brainstorm words is up, give each group three sheets of paper of different colors. Tell them that the red paper is for a word from their list they think all the other groups would also have thought of—a common word. The green paper is for a word they don't think any other group will have thought of—a unique word. On the yellow paper, they will write the word from their list that they think is most interesting and which they would like to learn more about. Have them write the word big enough to fill the whole sheet of paper because they are going to share that word with the whole class. Show students 10–15 pictures from the text. Give them 20 seconds to talk about each picture.

| ice | regurgitate | emperor |

5. Gather your students together and have each group show the word they have chosen as common, as unique, and as interesting. As they show the different words, help students determine how well they predicted which of their words were common to many other trios and unique to their trios. Ask each trio to explain their reasoning for which of their words was most interesting.

6. Give the students the text you want them to read.
    Have them read the text together and put a * on each word they predicted that actually did occur in the text.

7. After reading, have the trios write five or six words they wish they had thought of.
    When they have finished reading the text, have trios decide on five or six words they should have guessed but didn't. Have them add these words to the brainstormed list they made before reading. Gather the class and lead students in a discussion about which words did occur and their reasons for choosing five or six words they wish they had guessed.

8. Have students use the vocabulary words to write some things they learned.
    End the lesson by having each student write two or three sentences summarizing what they read. Each sentence must use at least two of their words.

Imagine that throughout the school year, you do a PPC lesson every week or two when your students are about to read some informational text with lots of pictures. By the end of the year, all your students will be in the habit of looking at pictures and thinking about what words will be used to talk about what they see in the pictures. Many times, they will be able to associate words they know with the pictures. Other times, they will ask themselves questions:

"What is that funny looking animal?"

"Why does the sign say 'Danger. Keep out'?"

"Why are all the people dressed in those funny clothes?"

Informational text contains pictures to capture our interest and help us access and connect relevant vocabulary. PPC lessons help students make maximum use of pictures when they are reading on their own.

English Language Learners

Think about all the vocabulary your students learning English will be adding as they talk about the pictures with two of their classmates and then read the text. If you spread your English language learners out in the trios and provide them with empathetic, supportive peers, they will feel secure and comfortable in using their English speaking skills.

Three Read-Aloud Words

In Chapter 2, you learned how important your read-aloud is in motivating students to read and how you can use the read-aloud time to expand their meaning vocabularies. You can also use your read-aloud time to teach students how you figure out the meanings of words. Several studies have demonstrated the power of focused read-alouds on fostering vocabulary growth (Beck, McKeown, & Kucan, 2002; Juel, Biancarosa, Coker, & Deffes, 2003). In each study, teachers went beyond just reading books aloud. Before they read the books aloud, they selected a few words for which they felt many children would not know the meanings. After the book had been read aloud and discussed, teachers returned to those selected words and focused student attention on them.

To maximize vocabulary growth from reading, choose one short piece each week and use that book, magazine, or newspaper article to teach your students how to learn new words from the reading. This lesson framework is called Three Read-Aloud Words, and here is how each lesson is carried out:

1. **Identify three "Goldilocks" words from a piece you are going to read aloud.**

   Any good book or article is going to have many words on which you could focus your attention. Narrowing the number of words you are going to teach to a reasonable number increases the chances that all your children will learn them. Beck, McKeown, and Kucan (2002) divided vocabulary into three tiers. The first tier includes words generally known by almost all children. *Boy, girl, jump, sad, laugh,* and *late* are examples of Tier 1 words. Many of your students will not know Tier 2 words but will need to know them. *Despair, exhausted, catastrophe,* and *proceeded* are Tier 2 words. Tier 3 words include less common, subject-area specific, and technical words. *Languid, ratio, constitution,* and *igneous* are examples of Tier 3 words. Beck and other experts suggest that we focus our time and energy in teaching Tier 2 words for vocabulary development. Some people refer to the Tier 2 words as "Goldilocks" words because they are not too well known, not too obscure, but hopefully "just right" for your students.

   As you begin to select your three "Goldilocks" words from the piece you are going to read aloud to your students, you will probably find a lot more than three possibilities. Narrow it down to three by considering the usefulness and appeal of the words to your children and how well the words are defined by the context and pictures. You might also choose a word because it has a word part (prefix, suffix, or root) you want your students to notice and analyze.

   Once you have chosen the three words, write them on index cards. For this example lesson, we are going to imagine that you have chosen an article from *Sports Illustrated Kids,* and the three words you chose to focus on are *overpowered, resurgent,* and *squandered.*

2. **Read the text the first time, making no reference to the three chosen words.**

   The first time you read anything aloud should always be for enjoyment and information. Read the piece aloud as you normally would, stopping from time to time to ask questions that will engage your students in the text, but without doing anything in particular about your chosen words.

3. Show the three words to your students.

After reading and enjoying the piece, show your students the words on index cards, one at a time. Have your students pronounce the words, but do *not* let anyone share any meanings. This may feel quite counterintuitive. As teachers, we are used to giving students meanings for words or asking them for meanings they know. However, when doing Three Read-Aloud Words, you want your students to discover that they can learn new words from their reading by thinking about the context along with any pictures or known word parts. If you let anyone tell what a word means, you have defeated your purpose of demonstrating how the students can acquire new meanings from their reading. If one of your students responds to a word by saying, "I know what *overpowered* means," your response should be, "I am so glad you think you know, but wait to tell us until we get to *overpowered* in the article!"

4. Reread the text and have the children stop you when you read each of the words.

Put the index cards with your three chosen words where your students can clearly see them. Now read the text to them again. On this second reading, do not stop to discuss pictures or engage the children with questions. When you come to one of the chosen words, some of your children are sure to notice and signal you. Tell students to stop you by shouting, "Stop!" and the word (for example, "Stop! *Overpowered*!"). No hand raising allowed in this activity!

When they signal you, stop reading and use the context, pictures, and word parts to explain each word. If words are repeated more than once, let the children stop you each time and see whether any new information is added to their understanding of the word. Here is an example of the context in which each word occurs and how to model figuring out the meaning of each word.

The word **resurgent** occurs in a sentence that explains that two batters scored four times and that the resurgent Yankees had won nine of their last 11 games. This context, along with the meanings of word parts the children know—**re** and **surge**—lets you conclude that the word **resurgent** means "coming back."

For **overpowered,** you can again use the context and the meanings of word parts—**over** and **power**—to determine that **overpowered** means "won the game by being much stronger."

> Alex Rodriguez homered twice and drove in five runs. The Yankees **overpowered** Pittsburgh for their sixth consecutive victory. (*Sports Illustrated Kids,* June 11, 2007, p. 2)

Squandered has no word parts to help, but the children conclude from the context that Clippard's team was in the lead but gave it up by walking two batters and then letting the next players get hits. **Squandered** means "wasted," "lost," or "gave up."

> Clippard quickly **squandered** the lead. He walked two in the fourth and gave up a two-run double that put Pittsburgh up 6–5. (*Sports Illustrated Kids,* June 11, 2007, p. 2)

5. **Help your students connect their own experience to the three words.**

Once you have finished reading, stopping each time one of the chosen words occurs, focus again on each word and ask a question that helps children connect their own experience to the text. For these words, you might ask students:

> "Can you think of a time when a team you were on or a favorite team was **resurgent**?"

> "Have you or a favorite player ever overpowered someone or been **overpowered** by someone?"

> "What could you **squander** in addition to the lead in a game?"

Let students turn and talk with each other for a minute after you ask each question. Then let them share their connections with these three words.

6. **Display the title and the three word cards somewhere in the room.**

After you have introduced these three words and modeled for the children how context, pictures, and word parts are helpful in figuring out meanings for new words; assisted the children in connecting these to their own experiences; and given them an opportunity to use these words to retell the text, display these words someplace in the room. You may want to copy the article or cover of the book and display the three index cards next to it. Tell your students that you and they are going to be on the lookout for these words in books and conversations and that they should try to use the words at school and at home. Every time someone hears, reads, or uses one of these words, he or she can put a tally mark next to the word. The word with the most tally marks at the end of one week is the winning word! (Kids love competitions, especially if they cannot possibly be the loser!) Once you do this, contrive to use these words in your conversations with the children over the next several days. Congratulate them when they notice the word and allow them to put a tally mark next to the word. Soon you will notice that the students are trying to sneak these words into their talk—exactly what you are aiming for! Once your students are alert to these words, ask them to listen for the words and to try to use them in their home environments. Let them report any instances of these words in their home environments and add tally marks to the appropriate words.

Read-Aloud Words Posters

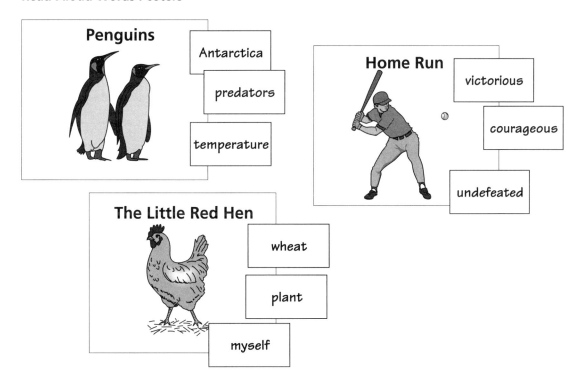

Word Detectives

Word Detectives is a lesson framework you can use to have your students work together to figure out new word meanings. Here are the steps in a Word Detectives lesson:

1. From a text your students are going to read, choose six words your students are unlikely to have meanings for and for which meaning can be figured out using context, pictures, and morphology. Include a word or two that students are familiar with but that have different meanings in this text.

2. Seat your students in trios—with an advanced, average, and struggling reader in each trio.

3. Show students the six words and have them pronounce each word, but do not let anyone suggest any meanings.

4. Have each person in the trio write two of the words on tiny sticky notes.

DDT	eyries	ornithologist
stoop	alarmed	fledglings

5. Give trios one copy of the text and have the trio read the text together.

6. Their first job as detectives is to find each word and place their sticky note close to the word.

7. Each detective trio should then use the clues—context, pictures, or familiar word parts—to sleuth out the meaning of the mystery words.

8. Come together as a class and let detectives tell how they used the clues to solve the mystery.

Sticky Note Day

If you are doing the Three Read-Aloud Words and engaging your students in Word Detectives and PPC lessons, you are already doing a lot to help your students be alert to new words in their own reading. Your students will be in the habit of looking at the pictures and thinking about what words in the text these pictures relate to. They will know how the context of what you are reading often makes clear the meaning of a word and that familiar word parts also add to or clarify the meaning of that word. Just because they know how to use pictures, context, and word parts to figure out what unfamiliar words mean does not ensure they will use these strategies when they are reading independently. In fact, many struggling readers employ the "skip it" strategy when they come to a word they don't instantly recognize or have a meaning for. To get your students to use what they know about learning word meanings from their reading, designate one day each week as a "Sticky Note Day." At the beginning of their independent reading time, give each student one sticky note. Tell everyone to be on the lookout for one word that is new to them and that they can figure out the meaning of based on the pictures, context, and/or word parts. Explain to your students how you choose your Three Read-Aloud Words by looking for useful words that many of them probably don't know the meaning of but that they can figure out. Ask your students to be on the lookout during their reading for a perfect word to teach to the class. They should write that word on a sticky note and place the sticky note on the sentence in which they first see the word.

When the time for independent reading is over, gather your students together and let four or five volunteers tell their word, read the context, and/or share the picture or word parts that helped them with the meaning of that word. Do not let everyone share their words, because this would take more time than you have, and you want your students to be excited about finding new words—not bored with having to listen to 25 explanations! Assure your students that you will give them another sticky note next Thursday and that you will let other children share their findings with the class.

If you designate one day each week as Sticky Note Day, your students will get in the habit of looking for interesting new words and using the pictures, context, and word parts to figure out this word. Soon they will be doing this in all their reading—even when they don't have a blank sticky

Example of "Sticky Note" Sentence

The ozone layer forms a thin shield high up in the sky. It protects life on Earth from the sun's ultraviolet (UV) rays. In the 1980s, scientists began finding clues that the ozone layer was going away or being depleted. This allows more UV radiation to reach the surface. This can cause people to have a gr[ ]chance of getting too much UV radiation. [ ]UV can cause bad health effects like skin c[ ]damage, and get you sick easier.

depletion

note staring at them—and they will be on their way to adding exponentially to their vocabularies every time they read!

Result: Independent Word Learning

Imagine that every week throughout the school year you use the Three Read-Aloud Words strategy for one text you are including in your teacher read-aloud time. You choose "Goldilocks" words—words that will be useful to your students and that many of your students will not have meanings for. When your students stop you in the second reading because they hear one of the words, you model for them how to use context, pictures, and word parts to figure out the probable meaning of the new word. You give them an opportunity to use the words in speaking by having them "turn and talk" to a partner about their connections with these words. You display the words and challenge yourself and your students to "slip" these words into their conversations.

Every week or two, you give your students something to read, put them in trios, and use the Word Detectives lesson framework to get them to talk with each other about how you can use pictures, context, and word parts to figure out words. Every week or two, you use the PPC lesson framework to teach your students how they can use the visuals in a text to add words to their vocabulary. One day each week, you give your students a sticky note and challenge them to find a word they didn't know the meaning of and use their word-sleuthing skills to figure it out.

At the end of the school year, what have you done to increase the children's meaning vocabularies? The obvious answer is that you have provided direct instruction with several hundred words. In providing that instruction, you have implemented principles for effective vocabulary expansion described in Chapter 1.

- Pictures and other visuals help solidify word meanings.
- To truly own a word, you must use that word in talking and writing.
- A set of essential words, including subject-area vocabulary, should be directly taught.
- Because most new words are learned through reading, teacher read-aloud and independent reading time should be scheduled into every elementary student's day.
- Students should be taught strategies for learning new words independently from reading, including instruction in word parts, context, and effective use of the dictionary.

Perhaps the most important thing you have accomplished is not the teaching of these words. Students who participate regularly in Three Read-Aloud Words, Word Detectives, PPC lessons, and Sticky Note Day learn strategies for acquiring new words from their reading, which they can use independently for the rest of their lives.

chapter 6

Morpheme Magic

English is one of the most morphologically complex languages. For every word we know, there are six or seven other words we can attach meaning to if we are "morphologically sophisticated." *Morphology* refers to word parts—roots, prefixes, and suffixes—that

add meanings to words or change their grammatical function. Linguists estimate that about half of all new words we encounter are structurally related to other words (Anglin, 1993).

In the previous chapter, I suggested that you help students notice familiar word parts and use these along with context to figure out meanings for unfamiliar words. This chapter will suggest activities you can use to directly teach the prefixes, suffixes, and roots that are most useful to elementary students in figuring out word meanings. You can use any reading materials for your word-part instruction. Including some sports articles from magazines and your local newspaper will increase your students' interest and motivation.

Teaching Compound Words

Your goal in all morphology instruction is to get your students into the habit of looking at an unfamiliar word and asking the question, "Do I know any of the word parts?" Because compound words abound in English and because figuring out the meaning of a compound word by thinking about the meanings of the two words that make up the compound is a relatively easy task, begin your word-part instruction with compound words. Find an article in your local newspaper or in *Sports Illustrated Kids* that has several compound words and read that article to your students. For the first reading, don't focus on the compound words but only on the content of the article and what happened in the game. Choose an article about a team your kids care about and, if possible, one in which the favorite team wins! Next, reread the article, and this time, ask your students to stop you when they hear a compound word. Use the Three Read-Aloud Words procedure described in Chapter 5, but have students stop you by shouting, "Stop! *Compound*!"

After stopping for each compound word, write that word on the board and ask students to tell you the two words making up the compound and how these words add to the meaning of the compound word. Just as in our example, the meaning of some compounds will be familiar—such as **football, kickoff,** and **touchdown**. Other words may be less familiar, and the meaning of the words that make up the compound less obvious—for example, **shotgun** and **touchback**—and students may need to use the context of the article to infer the word meanings.

Next, put students in groups and give each group the sports section of the newspaper and a highlighter. Give them 12 minutes to find and highlight as many compound words as they can. When the time is up, let the groups share the words and explain what each means using prior knowledge and/or context.

Begin a compound bulletin board by having the groups divide up the task of writing the compound words on large index cards. Students should write the compound word on one side of the card in large letters with a marker. On the back of the card, have them write the sentence in which they found the word. While the groups work on this task, write the compound words from the article you read to them, along with sentences on the back on index cards. Attach all words to a compound bulletin board. Tell the students that for the next two weeks, everyone will be searching for compound words in everything they read. Provide lots of index cards and colorful markers. Ask students to initial and date each card before attaching it to the board so that everyone will know who found the word. Be sure to include some words you find during your teacher read-aloud. Take a few minutes each day to see what compound words were added to the collection. By the end of the two weeks, the compound board will look like a "collage" with new words on top of older ones. Don't worry if your compound board is crowded and messy. You have accomplished your goal of alerting your students to the pervasiveness of compound words and how they can learn new words by thinking about the meanings of the words making up the compounds and the context. You have also successfully launched your students on their word-part journey!

Compound Sort

While on the hunt for compounds, you may also want to provide more practice with compounds by having your students do a compound word sort. Put your students in groups and give them a list of compound words and some categories. Have the groups decide where each word belongs

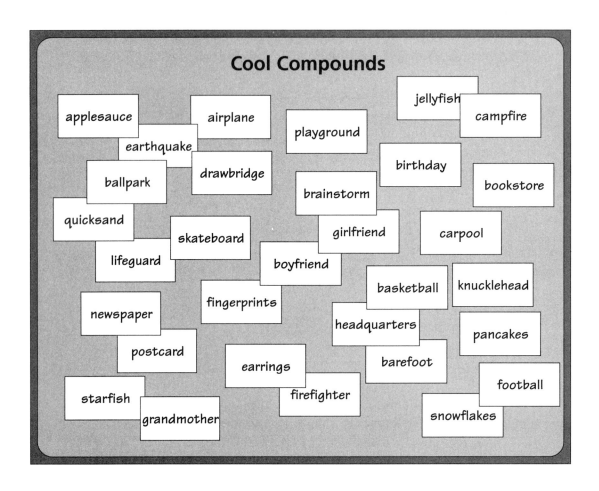

Cool Compounds

applesauce · airplane · playground · jellyfish · campfire · earthquake · drawbridge · birthday · bookstore · ballpark · brainstorm · quicksand · skateboard · girlfriend · carpool · lifeguard · boyfriend · basketball · knucklehead · fingerprints · newspaper · headquarters · pancakes · postcard · earrings · barefoot · starfish · firefighter · football · grandmother · snowflakes

and write it in the appropriate column. Here are some compound words that can be sorted into six categories.

Football	Basketball	Baseball/ Softball	Soccer	General Sports	Nonsports

afternoon	dugout	linebacker	somewhat
airplane	earring	lineman	somewhere
airport	earthquake	nationwide	southpaw
anyone	everybody	newspaper	speedball
anywhere	everywhere	nightcap	sweatshirt
backdoor	fastball	notebook	teammates
backstop	fingernails	offside	thunderstorm
ballpark	football	outcome	touchback
baseline	fullback	outfield	touchdown
baseman	goalkeeper	overtime	touchline
benchwarmer	goalpost	playground	turnpike
birthday	goaltending	quarterback	underdog
bookstore	goldfish	rainmaker	underhand
carpool	grandmother	scoreboard	upstairs
changeup	haircut	screwball	whatever
classmate	halfback	shootout	windup
cornerback	headache	shortstop	workshop
crossover	headlights	shotgun	wraparound
crosswalk	homework	shutout	yourself
daylight	infield	sidearm	
doubleheader	kickoff	sideline	
downtown	lifeguard	somehow	

Writing Compounds

In Chapter 1, several principles for vocabulary development were stated. One of these principles was:

> To truly own a word, children must use that word in talking and writing.

The major reason for putting students in groups to find and sort compound words is so they will talk to one another about these words, which helps you accomplish the speaking goal. Once you begin collecting compounds, do some quick-writes in which students use the compound board and any compound word sort to write something, using as many compound words as they can. Show the students that their writing can be silly by writing a few silly sentences yourself.

The knuckleheads ate applesauce at the ballpark.
The lifeguard saved his grandmother from the jellyfish.

Limit the time the students write to no more than five minutes, and then let them share their silly sentences. Students usually enjoy this silly writing more if they are allowed to write with a friend if they wish.

Teaching Common Prefixes

Four prefixes—**un, re, in,** and **dis**—are the most common and will help students figure out the meaning of over 1,500 words. Graves (2004) suggests teaching these prefixes to all elementary students. Teaching students to use prefixes and root words to add new words to their meaning vocabularies is important, but it is more complicated than teaching them to use the parts of compound words. In many prefixed words, the meaning of the word is not readily apparent by simply combining the meaning of the prefix and the root. Often, words begin with syllables that have the same spelling as prefixes but they are not prefixes. Knowing that **im** can mean "opposite" helps you build meaning for **impatient** and **improbable** but not for **imagine** or **immense**. Students need to learn the common prefixes, but they must also learn that those prefixes will not help them figure out the meaning of all words that start with those letters.

Teaching the Prefix **un**

Because words that begin with the prefix **un** are the most common and because students know a lot of words in which the prefix **un** appears, prefix instruction should probably begin here. Begin your prefix instruction as you began your compound word instruction—by reading something to your students that contains several **un** words. Use a high-interest newspaper or magazine article that contains several **un** words or write a paragraph describing something your students have experienced, perhaps a recent loss of your students' favorite team.

On Friday night, East High's **unbeaten** football team was **unable** to score against Jonesboro High's **unmerciful** defense. With only five seconds left, Jonesboro's kicker **unloosed** a 40-yard field goal to win the game, 3–0. East High's head coach was **unrestrained** in his praise for Jonesboro's team. "Their defense was our **undoing**! I'm **uncertain** how many years it's been since we played a game and didn't score at least one touchdown. That's all we needed to win, but we were **unsuccessful** every time we got the ball. I'm also **unhappy** that we kept getting **untimely** penalties that stopped our progress or gave them good field position. We didn't lose because we were **unlucky,** but because we were **unworthy**!"

After reading the article the first time for meaning, have the students listen again and stop you when you come to any **un** words by shouting, "Stop! *Un*!" Each time they stop you, talk with them about the words and help them see that **un** often changes a word to its opposite meaning. Write these words on large index cards with the sentence on the back and use them for the beginning of your **un** bulletin board.

Next, put students in groups and have them brainstorm as many words as they can that begin with **un** and in which **un** turns the word into the opposite. Have students use markers to write the word on one side of the card and pencil to write a sentence illustrating that word's meaning on the other side. When the time is up, let the groups share their words and use these cards to begin your **un** bulletin board.

Of course, you want students to hunt for **un** words as they did for compound words, but this hunt will be more complicated because in some words, **un** is not a prefix but only the first syllable. Using index cards of a different color, write several words in which **un** is not a prefix meaning "opposite"—for example, **uncle, understand,** and **uniform**. On the back of the card, write a sentence for each of these words. Attach these index cards to your **un** board and explain to students that they should use the white cards for words in which **un** turns a word into its opposite meaning and blue (or whatever color you have chosen) cards for any words they find that begin with **un** but in which **un** is not a prefix meaning "opposite" or "not." Just as with compound words, let the **un** collecting continue for two weeks and take a few minutes at the end of each day to talk about the new **un** words added and to read the sentences in which they were found. Model and remind students of this ongoing hunt by adding some **un** words that occur during your teacher read-aloud, including some in which **un** is just a syllable and not a prefix meaning "opposite." When your bulletin board is complete, have your students do some "silly writing" in which they have five minutes to use as many **un** words as they can. You may want to remind them of Alexander's terrible, horrible, no good, very bad day and suggest that they write about a bad day, real or imagined.

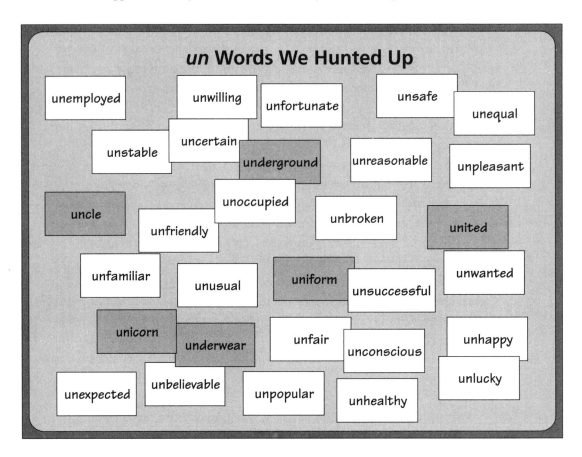

Teaching the Prefixes **in** and **dis**

Two other prefixes, **in** and **dis**, are also fairly common and also have the meaning of "opposite" or "not." The complicating factor in teaching these prefixes is that there are many words in which the prefix does not have the opposite meaning or in which the opposite meaning would not be clear to your students. To further complicate matters, the prefix **in** is spelled **i-l** before words beginning with **l** (**illegal, illogical**), **i-r** before words beginning with **r** (**irrational, irreversible**), and **i-m** before words beginning with **p** (**impossible, impatient**). To teach these prefixes, students probably need to be given a list of words to sort, rather than coming up with words on their own. Here is a list of commonly known words and four categories into which students should work in groups to sort them.

dis Prefix Meaning "Not" or "Opposite"	*dis* Not a Prefix	*in/im/il/ir* Prefix Meaning "Not" or "Opposite"	*in/im/il/ir* Not a Prefix

distance	illiterate	irrational	irresistible
illegal	impeach	irregular	displeased
innocent	incompetent	discourage	improper
discuss	discussion	important	impossible
dislike	impress	disobey	disconnect
illustration	disappear	impatient	impartial
dispute	impostor	invitation	distasteful
improve	impulsive	disturbance	immediately
impure	disaster	impossible	dissatisfied
disgrace	immeasurable	instrument	immigration
immigrant	include	incorrect	immune
distrust	insane	dishonest	distributor
increase	disorder	invite	disapproval
injury	inspire	disappoint	disappearance
informal	independent	illustrator	disagreement
disprove	inexpensive	irritation	disloyal
illogical	disagree	irresponsible	discrimination
incomplete	immortal	imitate	
discover	inadequate	immobile	

Teaching the Prefix **re**

Re, meaning "back" or "again," is another prefix that generates lots of words and that has many examples students know. Like **in** and **dis,** however, there are also a number of words that begin with **re** in which **re** is simply the first syllable and not a prefix. Put students in groups and have them sort **re** words into three categories.

re Prefix Meaning "Back"	*re* Prefix Meaning "Again"	*re* Not a Prefix

readjust	reelect	reopen	reread
reappear	refill	reorder	rerun
rearrange	refrigerator	reorganize	responsibility
rebound	refund	repaint	result
rebuild	refuse	repair	retire
recall	relax	repeat	return
receive	relay	replace	reunite
recess	relocate	replacement	review
recharge	remainder	replant	revolver
reconsider	remember	reply	reward
reconstruct	remodel	report	rewrite
recycle	remote	reporter	
reduce	rename	reproduce	

Teaching the Less Common Prefixes

Un, in, dis, and **re** are clearly the prefixes that generate enough useful words to merit teaching to elementary students. Here are some other prefixes that occur much less often. These prefixes are probably not worth a whole lesson, but it would be helpful to point them out to students when they occur during read-aloud or other lessons and alert students to their meaning. As with **un, dis, in,** and **re,** be sure students understand that not all words that begin with these letters will function as prefixes and in those cases, the prefix meaning will not help them understand the word.

in meaning "in"

> inside income indent indoors infield insight intake inland inmate

mis meaning "wrong (wrongly)"

> mistake misbehave misdeal misjudge mistrust mistreat misspell misprint misplace mislead misunderstood misfortune

non meaning "not"

> nonsense nonliving nonrenewable nonexistent nonessential nonstop

pre meaning "before"

> preview pregame prepay pretest precook preexisting preschool preteen preheat premature

en meaning "make" or "put"

> enjoy enforce enclose ensure enlarge enrich enlist enable encourage enroll enact endanger enrage endear

over meaning "over" or "too much"

> overpower overdo overcome overwhelm overjoyed overhand oversleep overtime overpass overnight overreact overweight

under meaning "under" or "below"

> underdog undergo underground underage underhand underline underwear underestimate underpass underweight underwater undercover

Just as with compound words, your purpose in teaching prefixes should be to help your students maximize the number of words they add to their vocabularies as they engage in reading throughout the day and across the curriculum. Your "big goal" is to help your students become morphologically sophisticated and to teach them that when they come to a big unknown word in their reading, they should ask themselves the key question, "Does this new word have any parts I know?" Students who combine the information provided by context and pictures with their knowledge of prefixes can add thousands of new words to their vocabularies.

Teaching Common Suffixes

Once students are in the habit of using the two words in a compound word and common prefixes to access word meanings, they can profit from instruction with the common suffixes. Most students easily learn the inflectional suffixes (also called endings)—**s, es, ed,** and **ing**—because they are so common in speech and writing. These endings do not change meaning or part of speech. Derivational suffixes, however, add meaning or change the grammatical function of the word. One complication with suffix instruction is that, unlike parts of a compound word or prefixes, suffixes often require spelling and pronunciation changes. **Funny** becomes **funniest, beauty** becomes **beautiful**, and **sign** becomes **signature**. These changes not only make suffix words difficult to spell but often result in young readers not recognizing the root word when a suffix is added. The most common and easy-to-understand suffixes that change meaning are **er** and **est,** meaning "more" and "most," **er** meaning "person or thing that does something," **ful** and **less**, and **able/ible**. Because they are the most common and easiest to understand, suffix instruction should begin with these suffixes.

Teaching **er** and **est**

Because **er** and **est** are so common, you can probably find a newspaper sports article that contains a lot of **er** and **est** words. If not, write a short paragraph describing a sports event your students care about. Use the previously described procedure of reading the article to your students for meaning first and then reading it again and asking students to stop you when they hear a word that ends in **er** meaning "more" or **est** meaning "most." As students stop you, write the word on an index card. If the word has a spelling change, be sure to point that out to your students and underline it on your index card.

Next, put your students in groups and let them hunt for words ending in **er** and **est** meaning "more" and "most." Students enjoy using highlighters to highlight these words. Once they have found and highlighted several words, have the groups divide up the words and write them on index cards, underlining any spelling changes and writing the sentence in which they found them on the back. Use the index cards you made, along with the ones your students made, to begin your **er/est** bulletin board. Encourage students hunt for **er/est** words meaning "more" and "most" in everything they read, and add these to the board.

Teaching **er** and Other Suffixes Meaning "Person" or "Thing"

The next common suffix that adds meaning to a word is **er** meaning "person" or "thing." Because this suffix is so common, you can probably use the now-familiar procedure of reading something to your students and having them identify the **er** words and then letting groups of students find **er** words meaning "person" and "thing" and writing them on index cards to begin a bulletin board. Be sure they underline spelling changes and write the sentence in which they found the word on the back. Once your **er** bulletin board is started, be sure to give the children a few weeks to hunt for this suffix in their reading. This hunting step is crucial because your big goal is not just to teach the suffix but also to establish the habit in your students of noticing new words in their reading and asking themselves whether the new word has word parts they know. Making the time for students to hunt for words in their reading is the transfer step in word-part instruction.

When your **er** bulletin board is complete, have your students do a quick-write in which they use as many **er** words as they can. Give them a time limit and permission to make their stories silly. Remember that to truly own a word, we must use it in talking and writing. The group work involved in identifying words in newspaper articles and categorizing words gives students a real reason to "speak" these words. Silly quick-writes provide a fun way of having students write the words.

There are three other suffixes that commonly indicate a person who does something. These are not common enough for your students to

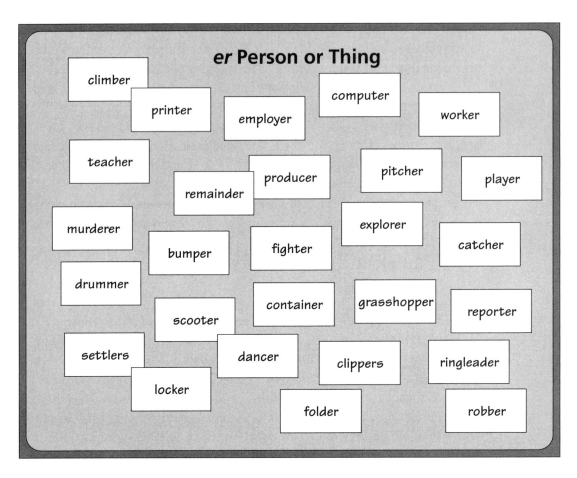

er Person or Thing

climber

printer

employer

computer

worker

teacher

producer

pitcher

player

remainder

murderer

explorer

catcher

bumper

fighter

drummer

container

grasshopper

reporter

scooter

settlers

dancer

clippers

ringleader

locker

folder

robber

hunt, but you could alert students to them by having groups categorize words with these suffixes. Here are some common **ian, or,** and **ist** words for students to categorize.

ist Person	*ist* Not a Suffix	*ian* Person	*ian* Not a Suffix	*or* Person	*or* Not a Suffix

actor	dentist	Italian	psychiatrist
alligator	director	journalist	psychologist
beautician	editor	librarian	razor
biologist	electrician	magician	resist
Californian	enlist	Martian	Russian
Canadian	exist	meteor	sailor
collector	favor	musician	scientist
colonist	flavor	odor	sculptor
color	florist	optimist	senator
comedian	governor	organist	specialist
conductor	guardian	persist	survivor
conqueror	historian	pessimist	tourist
counselor	Indian	pianist	typist
cyclist	insist	politician	visitor
custodian	inventor	professor	warrior

Teaching **ful** and **less**

Two other common suffixes that add meaning to words are **ful** and **less**. Some root words make new words with both **ful** and **less,** and the words take on an opposite meaning. **Hopeful** and **hopeless** are perhaps the best example of this. Other words combine with one but not the other, as in **beautiful** and **homeless**. Most students know a lot of words that end in **ful** and **less** and understand the meanings of these suffixes, so they are relatively easy to teach. To teach these suffixes in a quick and effective way, have students work in groups to decide which roots make a word with **ful**

Words with Suffix *less* Meaning "Without"	Words with Suffix *ful* Meaning "Full" or "Having"

arm	end	mercy	rest
beauty	fear	mouth	score
bottom	forget	pain	speech
breath	fruit	peace	spoon
care	harm	penny	thank
cheer	help	pity	thought
cloud	home	play	truth
color	hope	plenty	use
doubt	limit	power	waste
dread	meaning	price	wonder

and which with **less** and write them in the appropriate columns. Be sure students know some words can be combined with both and remind them of the **y** changing to **i** spelling change needed if the root word ends in **y**.

When the chart is complete, have students write sentences contrasting the words that have the same root and the opposite meaning in the same sentence. Give them an example or two to get them started:

We were **powerless** when we got hit by the **powerful** storm.

I was **hopeful** our team would win, but the other team was so good it was **hopeless**.

Teaching **able** and **ible**

The final suffixes that add meaning to words and that are relatively easy for students to understand are **able** and **ible**. Have students work in groups to sort words into four categories.

able Suffix Meaning "Able"	*able* Not a Suffix	*ible* Suffix Meaning "Able"	*ible* Not a Suffix

acceptable	distractible	miserable	suitable
adjustable	dishonorable	movable	syllable
adorable	eligible	permissible	terrible
affordable	enjoyable	possible	unavoidable
agreeable	excitable	predictable	uncomfortable
available	fashionable	preferable	undesirable
believable	favorable	profitable	unfavorable
breakable	flexible	questionable	unforgettable
capable	gullible	reasonable	unstable
comfortable	horrible	recyclable	unsuitable
compatible	impossible	reliable	usable
convertible	indescribable	resistible	valuable
corruptible	inseparable	respectable	vegetable
dependable	laughable	responsible	washable
desirable	likable	reusable	workable
digestible	lovable	sensible	

Teaching **ous**, **al**, and **y**

Ous, al, and **y** are common suffixes that don't change the meaning of words, but rather change the word's grammatical function or part of speech. Something that is **poison** is called **poisonous**. A problem for a **nation** is a **national** problem. A day with lots of **sun** is a **sunny** day. Have students work in groups to categorize the root words according to what suffix can be added to them. The students should write the whole word—root and suffix—in the appropriate column. Remind them of spelling changes some of these words will need.

ous Words	*al* Words	*y* Words

adventure	electric	juice	poison
ambition	fame	logic	politics
bump	fog	luxury	rain
bury	fun	magic	region
caution	fury	mountain	risk
chill	globe	music	rust
cloud	glory	mystery	spine
coast	grass	nation	stick
comic	grouch	nature	sun
continue	hair	navy	thirst
curl	hazard	nerve	tribe
danger	humor	nutrition	tropics
dirt	industry	option	water
dust	joy	person	wind

Writing **ous**, **al**, and **y** Riddles

Once the words are put into categories, have each group pick four or five words and write a riddle for the other groups to solve. Have the students write the riddle on one side of a card and the word that answers the riddle on the other side. Have them begin each riddle by telling which suffix the word ends with. Give them a few examples to get them started.

> I end in **ous**. I make you laugh when I am a story. What am I? (hilarious)

> I end in **y**. I make you want to get something to drink. What am I? (thirsty)

Teaching **ment**, **ance**, **ness**, and **tion**

Ment, ance, ness, and **tion** are common suffixes that don't change the meaning of words but rather change the word's grammatical function or part of speech. We try to **equip** our army with the very best **equipment**. The money we are **allowed** to spend each week is our **allowance**. When you feel **happy,** you are experiencing **happiness**. We hold **celebrations** to **celebrate** weddings and birthdays. Have students work in groups to categorize the root words according to what suffix can be added to them. Students should write the whole word—with root and suffix—in the appropriate column. Remind them of spelling changes some of these words will need.

ment Words	*ance* Words	*ness* Words	*tion* Words

accept	connect	engage	intervene	quest
act	construct	enjoy	introduce	ready
adjust	contradict	equip	invent	reduce
adopt	contribute	excite	invest	reject
advertise	convict	execute	isolate	rely
agree	correct	fair	kind	replace
allow	corrupt	fit	lazy	require
amaze	dark	forgive	locate	resist
annoy	develop	good	manage	restrict
appear	devote	govern	measure	rotate
argue	direct	great	migrate	sad
arrange	disagree	guide	move	select
assign	disappear	happy	mutate	settle
attach	disappoint	ill	open	ship
attend	distort	illustrate	pave	sick
attract	distract	impeach	pay	state
aware	disturb	improve	persecute	subtract
bitter	donate	indicate	place	treat
bright	educate	inflate	predict	weak
clear	elect	inject	prevent	
collect	employ	insure	produce	
command	encourage	interact	promote	
complete	endure	interrupt	punish	

Writing **ment**, **ance**, **ness**, and **tion** Riddles

Once the words are put into categories, have each group pick four or five words and write a riddle for the other groups to solve. Have the students write the riddle on one side of a card and the word that answers the riddle on the other side. Have them begin each riddle by telling which suffix the word ends with. Give them a few examples to get them started.

> I end in **tion**. We learned to do this in math. What am I? (addition)
>
> I end in **ance**. You might get this each week if you do your jobs at home. What am I? (allowance)

Teaching **ly**

Ly is the other suffix that occurs often enough to merit teaching to elementary children. Words that end in **ly** are often adverbs that modify verbs, adjectives, or sometimes other adverbs. Because students know a lot of **ly** words and because almost all words that end in **ly** are adverbs, you can use the procedure described earlier for **un** and **er**. Read an article to your students and have them stop you when you read a word that ends in **ly** by shouting, "Stop! *Ly*!"

Write these **ly** words on index cards and talk about how **ly** changes the way a word can be used in a sentence. Put students in groups and have them brainstorm some **ly** words to begin the **ly** board. They should write the word with a marker on one side of an index card and write a sentence with that word in pencil on the other side. Use cards with **ly** words from what you read to them and those brainstormed by each group to begin an **ly** board. Let students hunt for **ly** words in everything they read for a week or two. Because some words that end in **ly** are not adverbs—such as **silly, hilly,** and **family**—provide some index cards of a different color on which students can write these words. Be sure students write the sentence in which they found the word on the back of the card. This encourages them to look for **ly** words when reading and discourages them from just writing any **ly** words they can think of.

Every day, take a few minutes to talk about the meanings of the newly added **ly** words. Because these words often show action, they lend themselves nicely to pantomime games. Let volunteers choose a word from the board and pantomime that word. The person who correctly guesses the word can mime the next word if he or she chooses.

Teach Cognates to Accelerate Vocabulary Growth for English Language Learners

Cognates are words in different languages that have the same root. Teaching your English language learners to use cognates is one way of teaching them to look for familiar word parts. English, Spanish, and French share a huge number of cognates. The chart here lists Spanish and French cognates for common English words. To see whether there is a Spanish cognate for a less familiar English word, you can use the Find a Cognate database (www.angelfire.com/ill/monte/findacognate.html). Just enter the English word, and if there is a Spanish cognate, it will appear. When teaching students about cognates, be sure they always check the meaning with the context. There are some "false cognates," however, and they can lead to errors. If you read "*Está embarazada,*" you might assume she is embarrassed, while in fact, she is pregnant!

English	Spanish	French
accent	acento	accent
accident	accidente	accident
active	activo	actif
actor	actor	acteur
admire, admiration	admirar, admiración	admirer, admiration
admission	admisión	admission
adore	adorar	adorer
adult	adulto	adulte
agriculture	agricultura	agriculture
alphabet	alfabeto	alphabet
ambition, ambitious	ambición, ambicioso	ambition, ambitieux
animal	animal	animal
apartment	apartamento	appartement
April	abril	avril

(*continued*)

English	Spanish	French
arrange	n/a	arranger
arrive	n/a	arriver
artist	artista	artiste
attraction	atracción	attraction
bank	banco	banque
bicycle	bicicleta	bicyclette
biography	biografía	biographie
block	bloque	bloc
blue	n/a	bleu
calendar	calendario	calendrier
calm	calma	calme
cancel	cancelar	n/a
capital (n)	capital	capitale
captain (n)	capitán	capitaine
carpenter	carpintero	n/a
category	categoría	catégorie
center, central	centro, central	centre, central
change (n)	n/a	changement
character (attributes)	carácter	caractére (of an individual)
chocolate	chocolate	chocolat
color	color	couleur
comfortable	confortable	confortable
comic (adj)	cómico	comique
commercial (adj)	comercial	commercial
confidence	confianza	confiance
conflict	conflicto	conflit
construction	construcción	construction
continue	continuar	continuer
cousin	n/a	cousin
credit	crédito	crédit
culture	cultura	culture
dance	n/a	danser
December	diciembre	décembre

English	Spanish	French
decision	decisión	décision
defend	defender	défendre
democracy	democracia	démocratie
dentist	dentista	dentiste
department	departamento	département
desert (n)	desierto	désert
destruction	destrucción	destruction
detail (n)	detalle	détail
determine	determinar	déterminer
dictionary	diccionario	dictionnaire
dinner	n/a	dîner
direction/director	dirección/director	direction/directeur
economy	economía	économie
education	educación	éducation
elementary	elemental	élémentaire
energy	energía	énergie
error	error	erreur
excellent	excelente	excellent
except (conj)	excepto	excepté
exercise (n)	ejercicio	exercice
extreme	extremo	extrême
fault (n)	falta	faute
finish (v)	n/a	finir
friction	fricción	friction
fruit	fruta	fruit
function	función	fonction
gallon	galón	gallon
gas (not gasoline)	gas	gaz
general (adj)	general	général
government	gobierno	gouvernement
habit	hábito	habitude
history	historia	histoire

(continued)

English	Spanish	French
honor (n)	honor	honneur
hospital	hospital	hôpital
hotel	hotel	hôtel
human	humano	humain
idea	idea	idée
illegal	ilegal	illégal
imagine	imaginar	imaginer
impressive	impresionante	impressionnant
individual (n)	individuo	individu
insect	insecto	insecte
insist (v)	insistir	insister
invent	inventar	inventer
invite	invitar	inviter
jacket	n/a	jaquette
labor	labor	labour
lamp	lámpara	lampe
legal	legal	légal
letter (of alphabet)	letra	lettre
liberty	libertad	liberté
magnificent	magnífico	magnifique
mark	marca	marque
message	mensaje	message
minute	minuto	minute
motor	motor	moteur
music	música	musique
national	nacional	national
notice (v)	notar	noter
November	noviembre	novembre
number	número	nombre
object (v)	objetar	objecter
observe	observar	observer
opinion	opinión	opinion
palace	palacio	palais
parade	parada	parade

English	Spanish	French
part (n)	parte	part, or partie
pass (v)	pasar	passer
pharmacy	farmacia	pharmacie
planet	planeta	planète
plate	plato	n/a
poet	poeta	poète
politics	política	politique
practice (n)	práctica	pratique
prefer	preferir	préférer
prepare	preparar	préparer
president	presidente	président
pretend	pretender	prétendre
prevention	prevención	prévention
principal (adj)	principal	principal
process	proceso	procés
producer, product	productor, producto	producteur, produit
program (n)	programa	programme
protest (v)	protestar	protester
radio	radio	radio
respond	responder	répondre
restaurant	restaurante	restaurant
result	resultado	résultat
salad	ensalada	salade
science	ciencia	science
September	septiembre	septembre
solid	sólido	solide
soup	sopa	soupe
special	especial	spécial
table	n/a	table
telephone	teléfono	téléphone
television	televisión	télévision
urban	urbano	urbain
vacant, vacation	vacante, vacación	vacant, vacances
visit (n)	visita	visite

Teaching Common Roots

This chapter began by suggesting that you begin your word-part instruction with compound words. Compound words have two root words. Once your students begin to understand how prefixes and suffixes help them connect meanings to words, they enjoy working with roots to see how many words they can construct. Of course, you will want to start with the most common and predictable root or base words. The word *play* occurs in such related words as *replay, playground,* and *playoffs. Work* is part of many words, including *workers, workout,* and *workstation. Place* is another common base word, and students often know the meaning of *placemats, replace,* and *workplace. Light* occurs in many words, including *lightning, headlights,* and *enlighten. Form* is the root for almost 100 words, including *formation, deformity,* and *platform. Time* can be found in numerous words, including *timeout, overtime,* and *timekeeper. Fire* occurs in words such as *misfire, fireplace,* and *fireworks. Ball* is part of many compound words, including *meatball, eyeball,* and *ballpark.* Students enjoy building word trees. The root word is the root of the tree and the branches are all the words that share that root. Once students have constructed a tree, challenge them to write a paragraph using as many of the words on the tree as they can.

Greek and Latin Roots

There is disagreement among vocabulary experts in terms of teaching students Latin and Greek roots. It is true that these roots do contain clues to meaning, but the meaning relationships are often hard to figure out, and students might get discouraged if they cannot discover the meaning of a word based on the meaning of the root. Perhaps the most sensible way for elementary teachers to approach Greek and Latin roots is to be aware of them and to point out relationships when they think these will be understandable to most children. When encountering the word *spectacle,* for example, you might explain that a spectacle is something a person sees that is quite striking or unusual. Furthermore, you might point out that the root *spect* means "to watch" and invite the students

Word Tree

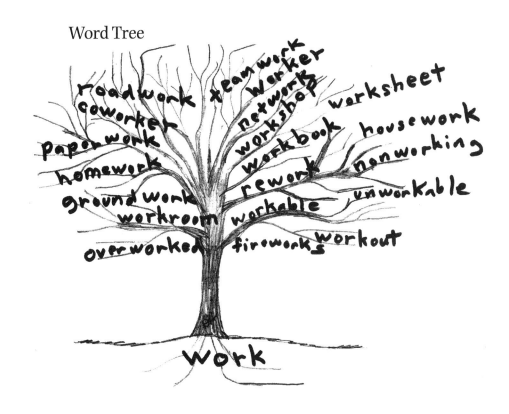

to think about how words they know, such as *inspection* and *spectators,* are related to this meaning. The word *constructive* could be explained as "helpful" or "building up" as opposed to *destructive,* which is "unhelpful" or "tearing down." Students might be told that the root *struct* means "to build" and asked to think about how other words they know, such as *structure* and *reconstruction,* are related to this meaning. The Greek and Latin roots chart below lists roots that occur most commonly in words elementary students read. When a word containing one of these roots occurs, it may be worth exploring the root meaning with your students.

Root	Meaning	Common Examples
dict	say	dictator, contradict, dictionary, unpredictable, verdict
duct	lead	duct, conductor, reduce, deduction, abduct, educate
fac/fec	do, make	factory, manufacture, benefactor, effect, defect
ject	throw	inject, reject, interject, object, subject, eject

Root	Meaning	Common Examples
loc	place	locate, location, relocate, dislocate, local
meter	measure	metric, kilometer, barometer, thermometer, diameter
micro	small	microphone, microscope, micromanage, microcosm
phon	sound	telephone, phonics, symphony, microphone, phonograph
photo	light	photograph, photography, telephoto, photosynthesis
port	carry, take	report, heliport, transportation, export, import, portable
press	press	impress, depression, pressure, express, oppression, compress
scrib	write	scribble, describe, prescription, subscribe, transcript
sens	feel	sense, sensitive, insensitive, sensation, consent, nonsense
spec	look	inspector, spectacle, respect, spectator, suspect, prospect
struct	build	structure, construct, reconstruction, instructor, destruction
tele	far	television, telegraph, telepathy, telephoto, telecommunication
tract	drag, pull	tractor, extract, contract, contraction, attract, subtraction
vis/vid	see	vision, revise, invisible, video, evidence
voc	voice, call	vocal, vocalize, advocate, vocation, convocation, provoke

The Magic of Morphemes

Morphemes—prefixes, suffixes, and roots—are the building blocks of English words. Morphemes are magical because when your students know how to do the tricks, they can turn one word into six or seven. Use the hunting, sorting, and writing activities in this chapter to turn all your students into morpheme magicians!

chapter 7

Building Vocabulary While You Teach Reading

Ask ten elementary teachers when they teach vocabulary, and nine out of ten will quickly respond, "Before children read."

Introducing new vocabulary before children read is so engrained in the minds of most elementary teachers that most of us never question its utility and effectiveness. Let's begin thinking about the proper role of vocabulary instruction during reading lessons by considering how effective traditional before-reading vocabulary introduction is.

In a typical reading lesson, the teacher selects eight to ten words that students might not know and introduces these words by writing them on the board, asking someone to tell what each word means, and asking someone else to use the word in a sentence. The students then read the selection containing these words and, hopefully, notice and connect meanings for the words introduced. In some classrooms, children then follow up the reading by looking up the vocabulary words and copying definitions. If there will be a test on these vocabulary words, students memorize the definitions they copied.

The questions we must ask ourselves are: "How effective is this traditional reading vocabulary instruction?" and "How many children who didn't already have these words in their meaning vocabularies will add these words based on these traditional activities?" If we are honest with ourselves, most of us know the answers: Traditional vocabulary instruction in which words are introduced, words are encountered in one text, and definitions are copied and memorized does little to move students toward acquiring those 1,000 to 3,000 new words they need to learn each year. Sometimes, tradition is a good thing. In the case of vocabulary instruction as part of reading lessons, however, tradition results in thousands of teachers wasting valuable time and energy in a daily routine that accomplishes little.

This chapter will suggest some radical changes in the way you approach vocabulary instruction during reading. As you read the chapter, think about this big question: "How can vocabulary instruction during reading be done in a way that will result in children who did not already know the meanings for the words adding many of the words to their meaning vocabulary stores?"

Choosing Which Words to Teach

When we shop for staples—shoes, for example—there are many, many choices. We know what we need, and we know that we can't afford all the shoes in the store. Perhaps we find a cute pair of black shoes, and then we remember how many pairs of cute black shoes we already have in our closets. We find some green shoes we like, and there are no green shoes in our closets, but then we wonder where we would wear the green shoes and what we would wear them with. We find some cute strappy sandals, but then we imagine walking on the four-inch heels and decide against them! We find a pair of very comfortable slip-on shoes but, on second look, they are really ugly! Finally, we settle on the perfect (we hope!) pair of shoes—stylish but comfortable, different from our other shoes, but not too different, and a perfect fit.

The first step in increasing the effectiveness of your vocabulary instruction is to be very picky about the words you teach. The biggest mistake teachers make in picking words is to select words solely because the words are unknown to their students. Sometimes we even feel compelled to introduce a word because we don't know what that word means, and if we don't know it, surely our students won't know it! Words whose meanings you have to look up are not apt to be words worth spending your vocabulary allowance on.

In suggesting which words to choose for Three Read-Aloud Word lessons, I suggested you focus on "Goldilocks" words, Tier 2 words that many students don't know but that will be useful to them. Once you have a list of possible "Goldilocks" words, think about the selection your students are going to read. How important is each word to comprehending the selection? If a word is a "Goldilocks" word but appears only once in the selection and is not essential to comprehending the selection, that word is probably like the green shoes—nice but not essential for this reading lesson.

Another factor to consider is whether the word has a word part you would like students to focus on. Does the word have a root, prefix, or suffix you have taught and that will remind students of the usefulness of asking the word-part question: "Does that new word have any word parts I know?" You might choose a "Goldilocks" word that is not crucial to comprehending the selection if that word allows you to refocus your students' attention on a common word part.

To maximize the effectiveness of vocabulary instruction during reading lessons, select each word by asking these questions:

- Is this a word most of my students don't have a rich meaning for?
- Is this a word my students need to know and could use in speaking and writing?

- Is this word essential to understanding the selection my students will be reading?
- Does this word have a word part I want to review or focus on?

When you choose your words based on these criteria, you know you have words worth the time and energy it will take to teach them.

In selecting the perfect words, try to include a few words students should be able to figure out for themselves based on the context, pictures, and word parts. After introducing the other words, tell your students that they will be word detectives for a few of the words. Use the Word Detectives activity described in Chapter 5 to have students sleuth out the meanings of the words. Give students sticky notes and have them pronounce and write the "mystery words" on them. Their first job as detectives is to find the words. When they locate the words, they should place the sticky notes on the words and look for clues to solve the mystery of what the words mean. After they read the selection, let students tell what meanings they figured out for the mystery words and how the context, pictures, and word-part clues helped them.

Introducing Vocabulary Before Students Read

When introducing vocabulary, try to implement the principles for effective vocabulary development outlined in Chapter 1:

- Vocabulary is learned best when it is based on real, concrete experiences.
- Pictures and other visuals help solidify word meanings.
- To truly own a word, you must use that word in talking and writing.

Look at the words you are planning to teach and think about these principles. Could any of the words be introduced using real or concrete experiences? Are there any pictures in the selection or readily available on the Internet that would make the concept clear? How could you quickly get students to make an initial connection with these words through speaking and writing? The way you introduce vocabulary words will vary depending on your resources and the particular words, but consider these possibilities.

Introduce Words with Real, Concrete, Hands-On Experiences

Providing real, concrete, hands-on experiences is often not possible during a reading lesson because of resource and time limitations. The feasibility of these real, concrete, hands-on experiences during math, science, art, music, and physical education is one of the major reasons for directly teaching a large number of the needed 1,000 to 3,000 new words while teaching these subject areas. But sometimes you can quickly provide something real or concrete, and asking yourself whether this is feasible each time you think about how to teach vocabulary increases the chances that it will happen.

Are there any objects in your classroom that are examples of the concept you are trying to introduce? What if the word you want to teach is **equipment**? Could you get together some things used to perform a certain task and explain that all these separate things together are your writing **equipment** or your painting **equipment**? If you wanted to introduce the word **flexible,** could you point to some objects in the room that are **flexible** and some that are not? What if the word were **essential**? What objects in your classroom are **essential** to learning?

Besides the physical objects in your room, you have another ready resource for providing quick and easy real experiences with new vocabulary words. You! Could you do anything to act out any of the words? Imagine, for example, that one of your "Goldilocks" words is **accidental**. Could you act out a scene in which you broke something and then had to explain to the owner that you didn't do it on purpose? It was **accidental**. What if the word were **envious**? Could you pretend that a teacher friend had won a marvelous vacation and then talk about how **envious** you are? What if the word were **pedestrian**? Could you act out crossing a street and declare your outrage when a car almost hits you and explain that **pedestrians** have the right of way at all crosswalks? Students love it when their teachers "ham it up," and most elementary teachers are natural actors. Not every vocabulary word lends itself to dramatization, but some do, and when you find yourself thinking about introducing a word that you could model, take the stage and have some fun!

Before moving on to thinking about how to provide visual experience with new words, consider these six words for which you could easily provide real experience.

equipment flexible essential accidental envious pedestrian

All these words have word parts you may want your students to think about. After showing them some equipment in your room, write the word **equipment** and ask your students whether this word contains any parts they know. Then help them see the **equip–equipment** relationship by using both words in a sentence, such as:

> To do anything, we need to **equip** ourselves with the necessary tools, which we call **equipment**.

You can do the same thing with **flex–flexible, accident–accidental,** and **envy–envious**.

> When we can **flex** or bend something, we say that thing is **flexible**.
> When something happens by **accident,** we say it was **accidental**.
> When you **envy** something, we say you are **envious**.

Essential and **pedestrian** also have word parts, but they are less obvious, and you may not want to point them out if your students are not ready to see the links. Most students who are not familiar with the word **essential** also don't know the word **essence**. **Ped** is the Latin root for "foot," so you might help children connect this word to something they know by using the familiar words **pedal** and **pedicure**. **Pedestrian** ends in **ian** as do many other words that name types of people, including **librarian, magician,** and **veterinarian**.

It is not always possible to provide real experience for words students will meet in their reading, but sometimes it is. Not all words have word parts you can point out to students to help them connect meanings, but many do. If every time you introduce vocabulary words before reading you utilize whatever real experience and word parts are available, you maximize the possibility that your students will actually add these new words to their vocabulary word store.

Take Your Students on Virtual Fieldtrips

New vocabulary generally falls into two categories. Many of the new words students meet are words for known concepts, such as **equipment, flexible, essential, accidental, envious,** and **pedestrian**. Perhaps most of your students have the concepts—just not the words.

> *equipment*—stuff you need for particular tasks
> *flexible*—bendable
> *essential*—you have to have it
> *accidental*—not done on purpose
> *envious*—wishing you had something someone else had
> *pedestrian*—person walking on a street

New words for known concepts are much easier to teach than new words for new concepts. For my first-graders in northern Florida, **escalator, park,** and **restaurant** were new words for new concepts. Not only did they not know the words, they had never experienced the things represented by the words. Children in Hawaii know all about **oceans,** but **deserts** and **canyons** are probably new concepts for Hawaiian children. Native American children living on reservations in Arizona certainly have the concepts for **deserts** and **canyons,** but probably not for **oceans** and **volcanoes.** Of course, providing concrete experiences for new words/new concepts is the best vocabulary introduction, but often this is impossible. When you can't provide real experiences, ask yourself whether there is any way to provide virtual experiences. One of the very best uses for Web technology is your ability to take your students on virtual fieldtrips. In some classrooms, equipped with SMART Boards and wired for the Internet, this virtual experience can be a part of each day's plan for vocabulary development. In other schools, you may have to plan to provide virtual experiences when you and your students can be scheduled into the media center or computer lab. Regardless of how accessible technology is in your classroom, your vocabulary introduction will be richer and more engaging if you make use of whatever virtual fieldtrips are possible.

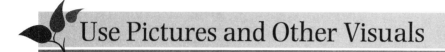

Use Pictures and Other Visuals

In addition to virtual fieldtrips, the Web provides every teacher with an endless source of visuals, including pictures, photos, and other graphic representations. Instead of bulky file folders full of pictures, savvy teachers today compile files of images stored on one slim disc. Because these images are so readily available and easily stored, you don't have to settle for just one picture—you can have a dozen or more images to represent a concept. Search for canyon images, and you will find pictures of both the Grand Canyon and a small unnamed canyon in the Himalayas. Having a variety of images for a new word that is also a new concept allows you to provide a richer introduction to that word and allows your students to broaden their concept from the start.

In addition to the wide range of visual images available on the Web, there is a source of readily available pictures often ignored when teachers think about introducing vocabulary. The text your students are going to read often contains illustrations that clarify the meanings of new words. The PPC lesson template described in Chapter 5 is a very efficient and motivating way to use the pictures in an informational text to introduce vocabulary and teach students how they can use pictures to build new word meanings. You can also use pictures in a more direct fashion by using a picture walk (Clay, 1991) to introduce new vocabulary before students read.

Use Picture Walks to Introduce Vocabulary

After you have decided on the words you want to introduce to students before they read, look at the pictures in the selection and see whether you can use any of them to build the vocabulary. Nouns represented by the pictures will be the most obvious possibilities, but pictures can also help you build meaning for verbs and adjectives. Imagine, for example, that the students are going to read a selection about volcanoes. The title page shows the volcano erupting and people fleeing the village. Four of your chosen vocabulary words—**volcano, eruption, evacuating,** and **terrified**—could be introduced using this one picture. Here is a script for the vocabulary introduction you might use for these four words:

"Boys and girls, let's look at the picture on the title page of our story and think about some vocabulary words that go with it."

(Teacher points to the volcano in the picture.)

"Does anyone know what we call this?"

(One student responds that it is a volcano.)

"Yes, that is called a volcano. A volcano is a...."

(Teacher shows an index card with the word **volcano** written on it and has everyone say the word **volcano**.)

"Show me a thumbs up if you have heard the word **volcano** before."

(Most students show a thumbs up.)

"Who can tell me anything you know about volcanoes?"

(Students share experiences with volcanoes, and teacher helps them access whatever knowledge they have by asking questions.)

"Has anyone ever seen a real volcano?"

"Have you ever seen a volcano in a picture or a movie?"

"Are there any volcanoes in our state?"

"Where could you go to see a volcano?"

(Teacher points to fire and debris coming out of volcano.)

"What is happening with this volcano?"

"What is coming out of the top?"

"Does the volcano always look like this, with lava and steam spouting out?"

"Does anyone know the word we use to describe a volcano that has lava and steam spouting out of it?"

(No one volunteers the word, so the teacher shows students the word **eruption** written on an index card.)

"When fire and debris spout out of the top of the volcano like this, we call that an eruption. Everyone say **eruption**."

(Students chorally pronounce **eruption**. Teacher supplies a "kid-friendly" definition of **eruption**.)

"Do you recognize any familiar word parts in the word **eruption**?"

(Students say that they know the **tion** part. Teacher writes the word **erupt** under **eruption** and uses the two words in a sentence.)

"This volcano is erupting. When a volcano erupts, we call that an **eruption**. **Erupt** and **eruption** are related words, just like **collect** and **collection**. If you collect baseball cards, you call this your baseball card…."

(Teacher pauses, and students quickly supply the word **collection**. Teacher gives a few more examples of **tion** words students know.)

"When we connect two things, we call this a…."

"When someone interrupts us, we call this an…."

(Teacher has students pronounce **eruption** one more time and asks them what **eruption** means. Students respond that **eruption** is what you call it when the lava and steam come out of the volcano. Teacher then directs their attention to the people in the picture.)

"Now look at the people. What are they doing?"

(Students respond that they are leaving, running away because the fire is dangerous. Teacher shows the index card with the word **evacuating**.)

"When people leave a place quickly because it is dangerous, we say they are evacuating. Everyone say **evacuating**."

(Students chorally pronounce **evacuating**.)

"We don't have to evacuate our town because of volcanoes, but sometimes we do have to evacuate because of something else that is very dangerous."

(Students immediately think of hurricanes and how they have had to evacuate their homes along the coast and go inland when a strong hurricane was coming. They eagerly share their experiences with hurricanes, and the teacher encourages them to use the new word **evacuating** to describe the very well-known concept of leaving their homes when a hurricane approaches.)

> "There is one more word we can use this picture to help us build meaning for. Look at the faces of the people who are evacuating because the volcano is erupting. Show me with your faces what their faces look like."

(Students eagerly mimic frightened expressions and explain that the people look like this because they are worried and scared and frightened.)

> "Exactly. They are worried and scared and very frightened. Here is a word that means not just a little scared and frightened but very, very scared and frightened."

(Teacher shows the word **terrified,** and students pronounce it.)

> "Were you terrified when you had to evacuate because the hurricane was coming? Have you ever been so scared or frightened by anything that if someone looked at your face he or she would say you were terrified?"

(Students eagerly share experiences of being really frightened. Teacher responds by using the word **terrified** to describe their feelings.)

> "I bet you were terrified when you watched that scary movie all by yourself."

> "I would be terrified, too, if I were camping and I saw a bear outside my tent."

In this Picture Walk example, the picture on the title page of the book provided visual support for the introduction of four vocabulary words. Many times, you may want to use several different pictures on different pages to introduce vocabulary. Imagine that your students are about to read an informational selection about animals. You have chosen several animal names to introduce to your students along with the word **habitat**. Your Picture Walk introduction might sound like this:

> "Boys and girls, look at the animal on this page. Do you know what this animal is called?"

(If a student names the animal, teacher agrees. If not, teacher continues.)

"This animal is called a buffalo."

(Teacher shows the word **buffalo** and has the students pronounce it. To get them to use the word **buffalo,** you ask them to compare a buffalo to another animal they know. Teacher continues.)

"In what ways does the buffalo look like other animals?"

(Students respond.)

"The buffalo has horns like a deer."

"The buffalo has hair like a horse."

"The buffalo has hooves like a cow."

"Very good. Now look at the animal on this page. Can anyone name this animal?"

You continue drawing students' attention to all the animals whose names you have chosen to introduce. For each one, you turn to the page with the picture of the animal and ask whether anyone knows the name. If someone knows the name, you acknowledge that and show the index card with the animal name on it and have everyone pronounce the name. You then provide students an opportunity to explore the attributes of this animal and use the animal name by asking them to compare the animal to other animals they know. After comparing each animal, tell students that they will learn lots more about the animal when they read about it and they will share that information after reading. It is not necessary to introduce all the animal names in the book— only the ones you think many of your students don't know.

To introduce the word **habitat,** draw students' attention to several pictures in the book that show where each animal lives. Show them the word **habitat** on an index card and tell them that an animal's habitat is where that animal lives. Let students describe the habitat for the pictures you are looking at by starting each sentence with the animal's name and the word **habitat**:

"The buffalo's habitat is the...."

"The giraffe's habitat is the...."

"The peacock's habitat is the...."

When you do a Picture Walk with students, you make use of the pictures in the selection to connect new words to old concepts and to build new concepts. For many of the students about to read the story about the volcano, the words **volcano** and **eruption** were new words for new concepts. Most students had experienced evacuating and feeling terrified. For them, the words **terrified** and **evacuating** were new words for known concepts. For students who have no experience with the animal names you introduced, these words would be new words for new concepts. Because most students have the concept of "the place where you live," the word **habitat** is probably a new word for a known concept.

Real and Visual Word Connections—Essential for English Language Learners

Using real and virtual experiences and visuals to introduce vocabulary is important for all children, but it is critical for children who are learning English. The majority of the words English language learners need to learn are new English words for those concepts they already know in their native languages. Using real and virtual experiences and pictures allows your students who are learning English to connect what they know because they can see the concept being taught. Whenever possible, ask your English language learners to tell you the word in their language. Unfortunately, even kid-friendly definitions are not apt to be very informative for children learning English because although they may have the concept, they may not know many of the words you use in your explanation. If you have English language learners in your classroom, redouble your efforts to find or create a real, virtual, or visual introduction to new meaning vocabulary.

For Teaching Vocabulary, Pictures Are Worth 1,000 Words

The "Goldilocks" vocabulary you choose to introduce to your students is always apt to be a combination of new words for new concepts and new words for old concepts. Because your students have had different experiences, lived in different places, watched different videos, and read different books, words that are new words for new concepts for some of your students will simply be new words for old concepts for other students. Regardless of which type of word you are introducing, pictures, along with real and virtual experience, provide a rich and engaging introduction to new words.

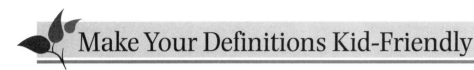

Make Your Definitions Kid-Friendly

Real, virtual, or picture experience is always required when introducing new words that are also new concepts for your students. When the words you want to introduce to students are new words for concepts they already know, you can introduce them by providing kid-friendly definitions. In *Bringing Words to Life* (Beck, McKeown, & Kucan, 2002), a splendid book on teaching vocabulary, the authors contrast dictionary definitions with what they call "student-friendly explanations." They cite dictionary definitions, such as "one associated with another," "appearance or feeling that misleads because it is not real," and "break up; split," and ask the reader how helpful these definitions would be if they did not already know the meanings for the target words: **ally, illusion,** and **disrupt** (pp. 36–37).

The authors explain that dictionary definitions are often unhelpful because space limitations require them to be concise and general. Because dictionary definitions are so brief and nonspecific, students who don't already know the meanings of the words are often misled. If **disrupt** means "break up" or "split," your students might think they could disrupt a candy bar to share with a friend! If **erode** means "eat away," this sentence written by a student to use **erode** in a sentence makes perfect sense!

My family likes to erode on weekends.

Rather than present students with dictionary definitions, Beck, McKeown, and Kucan suggest providing student-friendly explanations that characterize the word and explain meanings in everyday language. For **ally,** instead of the vague dictionary definition, "one associated with another," their student-friendly explanation is:

"someone who helps you in what you are trying to do, especially when there are other people against you" (p. 36)

For **illusion,** instead of "appearance or feeling that misleads because it is not real," the authors suggest:

"something that looks like one thing but is really something else or is not there at all" (p. 37)

For **disrupt,** instead of "break up; split," their student-friendly explanation is:

"to cause difficulties that stop something from continuing easily or peacefully" (p. 37)

Student-friendly explanations are one way to introduce your students to words for which they already have a concept and only need to connect the new word to the old concept. With any type of vocabulary introduction, it is crucial that students have a chance to use the word for which you have provided an explanation. The easiest way to ensure that your students are actively involved in your vocabulary introduction is to seat them in "talking partners" and have them "turn and talk." After providing your student-friendly explanations for **ally, illusion,** and **disrupt,** for example, have the students connect their experiences to these words by giving them a "turn and talk" task.

"Turn and talk to your partner about an ally you have had—someone who helped you in something you were trying to do, even if other people were against you."

"Turn and talk to your partner about an illusion you have seen—something you saw and thought was one thing but it turned out to be something else or something you thought you saw but really wasn't there."

"Turn and talk to your partner about something that happened that disrupted an activity you were engaged in. Did the rain ever disrupt your ball game? Did a family emergency ever disrupt your vacation plans?"

To develop deep knowledge of a word, it is often helpful to think of what a word is not. After introducing the word **ally,** you could have your students turn and talk and start their sentence with:

"A person is not an ally when…."

After all your vocabulary words are introduced, you can have students do some "turn and talk" tasks that get them to think about all the new words. Ask the talking partners to choose two of the vocabulary words that go together in some way. Give them a minute to do this and then ask them which two words they chose. See whether anyone can guess how these words go together. Children also enjoying making up sentences with their words and telling them to the class, leaving blanks for the word. Give the talking partners one minute to compose a sentence and then let them share their sentences with the class and see who can guess the vocabulary word they left out.

Carol was my _____ when she helped me clean my room.

We thought we saw a monster in the window, but it was an _____.

It rained a little at the ballpark, but not enough to _____ the game.

Many vocabulary words are new words for known concepts. When you are introducing vocabulary that most of your students already have concepts for, you can give them kid-friendly definitions for those words and then provide an opportunity for them to connect the words to their experience by giving them a quick "turn and talk" task. To find kid-friendly definitions, you can go to vocabulary.com. There you will find an example and, often, one students can relate to. Put **ally** in the search window, and the first thing you see is:

If you have an *ally,* you have someone who is on your side, like a more experienced teammate who is your *ally* in convincing the coach to give you more playing time.

Rivet is an activity I created one day while sitting in the back of a classroom watching a student teacher try to introduce some vocabulary words to her students. The vocabulary the student teacher was introducing was important to the story, and the words were words most of the students had concepts for; they only needed to learn the words. The student teacher was diligently writing the words on the board, giving kid-friendly definitions, and having students access meanings for the words and relate them to each other. Unfortunately, the students were not particularly interested in the words, and their attention was marginal at best. After the words had been introduced and the students began to read the selection, many of the struggling readers couldn't decode them, much less associate meaning with them. Rivet was conceived that day and has since saved many a student teacher from the dreaded experience of having taught some words that no one seemed to have learned!

When using Rivet to introduce vocabulary, select the words as you always do. Choose words that many of your students don't know but need to know, as well as words that are important to the selection. Also include the names of important characters, especially if these names will be difficult for your struggling readers to decode. Sometimes, as in this lesson, you may want to include a two-word phrase if it is very important to understanding the selection. The following Rivet activity is based on the book *Arturo's Baton* by Syd Hoff. Begin the activity by writing numbers and drawing lines on the board to indicate how many letters each word has. The board at the beginning of this Rivet activity would look like this:

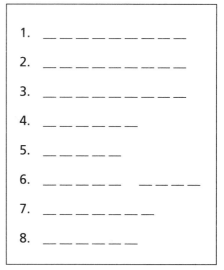

1. _ _ _ _ _ _ _ _ _
2. _ _ _ _ _ _ _ _ _
3. _ _ _ _ _ _ _ _ _
4. _ _ _ _ _ _
5. _ _ _ _ _
6. _ _ _ _ _   _ _ _ _
7. _ _ _ _ _ _ _
8. _ _ _ _ _ _

For each word, fill in the letters in order one at a time. Tell the students that they are allowed to "shout

out" in a Rivet activity and that they should shout the word as soon as they think they know it. Pause briefly after you write each letter to see whether anyone can guess the word. Students are not guessing letters but are trying to guess each word as soon as they think they know what it is. Most students will not be able to guess the word when the board looks like the first example. But after you add a few more letters, as in the second example, many will have some good guesses.

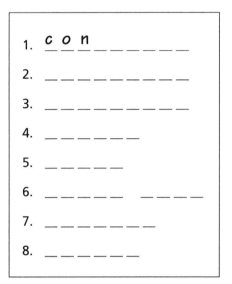
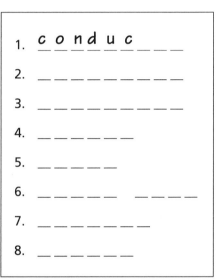

Once someone has guessed the correct word, finish writing the word, have everyone pronounce **conductor,** and ask whether anyone knows what the word **conductor** means. For **conductor,** students may say that a train has a conductor. Accept the answer and ask whether anything besides a train has a conductor. If students suggest orchestra or band, acknowledge those answers and then ask whether they know any other meanings for the word **conductor**. If you are studying electricity in science, someone may think of that meaning for conductor. As you introduce each word, ask questions to elicit the total knowledge of the class about each word, but don't give away how the word is used in the story.

After eliciting all the associations anyone in the class has with **conductor,** begin writing the letters of the second word, pausing for just a second after writing each letter to see whether anyone can guess the word.

Box 1 (left):

1. c o n d u c t o r
2. o r c h _ _ _ _ _ _
3. _ _ _ _ _ _ _ _ _
4. _ _ _ _ _ _
5. _ _ _ _ _
6. _ _ _ _ _   _ _ _ _
7. _ _ _ _ _ _ _
8. _ _ _ _ _ _

Box 2 (right):

1. c o n d u c t o r
2. o r c h e s t r a
3. _ _ _ _ _ _ _ _ _
4. _ _ _ _ _ _
5. _ _ _ _ _
6. _ _ _ _ _   _ _ _ _
7. _ _ _ _ _ _ _
8. _ _ _ _ _ _

The attention of all the students is generally riveted (thus the name Rivet) as each letter appears, and with a few more letters, many students will guess the word.

Once the word **orchestra** is completed and pronounced, ask students what they know about an orchestra. Is it different from a band? Have they ever seen an orchestra? Do they know anyone who plays in an orchestra? Now that you have the word **orchestra,** ask students how they think **conductor** and **orchestra** go together. Help students to see that in this story, the meaning of conductor is probably going to be the person who directs the orchestra.

Continue in this fashion until all the words have been completely written and correctly guessed. Here is what the board will look like when all words are introduced.

After writing each word and having the students pronounce the word, ask questions to elicit all the possible meanings of the words and any relationships students see between

Box 3 (bottom right):

1. c o n d u c t o r
2. o r c h e s t r a
3. T o s c a n i n i
4. A r t u r o
5. b a t o n
6. w o r l d   t o u r
7. p a j a m a s
8. c a n c e l

words. In this lesson, one student commented, "What do pajamas have to do with anything?" The teacher responded, "That is a strange word here, but it turns out it is an important word in the story."

Next, you want students to use the words. To get students to process words and use them in speech, ask them to make a prediction about something they think will happen in the story. Their prediction must use at least two of the vocabulary words. Have partners turn and talk to create their prediction together and then encourage them to share their predictions with the class. Write five or six of their predictions on the board, underlining the vocabulary words introduced.

The orchestra went on a world tour.

The conductor was Toscanini.

Arturo Toscanini was the conductor of the orchestra.

They had to cancel the concert because the orchestra wore their pajamas.

Toscanini forgot his pajamas when he took the orchestra on a world tour.

If the children fail to use some of the words in their predictions, prompt them to think about how those words might fit into the story. After asking them how the baton fits into the story, you might get these predictions:

Toscanini needed the baton to conduct the orchestra.

Toscanini got mad and threw the baton at the orchestra so they had to cancel the show.

Children generally enjoy combining the important words and making predictions. Sometimes their predictions actually happen, and they are quite pleased! The important thing is not whether the predictions are right or wrong. What matters is that your students are using the key vocabulary and anticipating how these words might come together to make a story.

When you have some predictions (six to eight is plenty), have the students read the selection to see whether any of the predictions were true. After the students have read the selection, ask them once again to use the key words to write some true things that happened in the story. Each sentence must include at least two of the words. Their sentences written after reading might include:

Arturo wanted to cancel the concert because he lost his baton.
Toscanini was Arturo's dog, and he found the baton.
Arturo decided he didn't need a baton, and he went off on a world tour.

Rivet is a very motivating way to introduce vocabulary when the words that need to be introduced are words most of your class has concepts for and some of your students have some meanings for. Children pay attention to the words as the words are being written because of the "hook" of trying to guess the word before anyone else does. They actively process the words by talking with their partners to create a sentence that uses at least two of the words and that predicts what might happen in the story. After reading, they use the words to write a sentence about what actually happened in the story using at least two of the words.

Sometimes the students are even more motivated when the teacher sets up a competition between the teacher and the class. In "Rivet versus the Class," if the students guess the word before the final letter is written, the class gets a point. If no one guesses the word before the teacher writes the last letter, the teacher gets a point. The class is always delighted when they beat the teacher, and if they guess every word, they declare it a shutout!

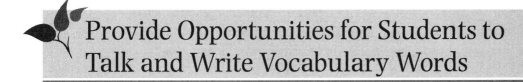

Provide Opportunities for Students to Talk and Write Vocabulary Words

If you introduce reading vocabulary using activities such as the ones suggested in this chapter, you have taken a huge beginning step in helping children add these words to their vocabulary stores. Remember, however, that to truly own the words, students must have multiple and varied encounters with those words, and they must use the words in talking and writing. One huge obstacle to children adding words introduced during reading lessons to their vocabulary stores is that the important vocabulary for one reading selection is not apt to occur again in future reading selections. You can use the structured discussion formats described in Chapter 3 to provide opportunities for your students to talk to each other using the new words. As your students work in small groups to list, group, and label words; decide how two words go together; choose words to complete blanks in sentences; decide on skits so others can guess a word; or complete A–Z charts, they are speaking the words. Quick-writes described in Chapter 4 provide opportunities for students to use the new words in writing.

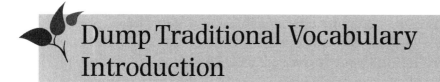

Dump Traditional Vocabulary Introduction

Sometimes tradition is a good thing—but not for teaching vocabulary during reading lessons. We have all sat through many hours of word introductions where students tell meanings and put words in sentences. For many of us, vocabulary instruction calls up memories of copying and memorizing definitions. When we think about it, we realize that this kind of vocabulary instruction cannot really teach students new word meanings that they will incorporate into their listening/reading/speaking/writing vocabulary stores. But the tradition is so pervasive that we often continue it without thinking about it. Vocabulary introduction does not have to be tedious and boring— for students or teachers! Buck tradition! Incorporate the activities in this chapter into your reading lessons. Your students' vocabularies will grow, and you and the students will look forward to vocabulary time!

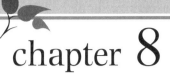

chapter 8

Building Vocabulary While You Teach Math

Every day in every elementary classroom, teachers spend 45 to 60 minutes teaching math. Like all subject areas, math has its own

vocabulary. In the early grades, this vocabulary is deceptively simple. Children learn to **count forwards** and **backwards,** learn the names of the **numbers** and how to **add** them and **subtract** them, learn that a **shape** with **three sides** is a **triangle** and that a perfectly round shape is a **circle,** and learn to **measure** things, including how to measure time and money.

The bold words in the previous paragraph are the "deceptively" simple vocabulary. Often, teachers take for granted that children know the meanings of such words as **count, forwards, backwards, numbers, add, subtract, shape, three, sides, triangle, circle,** and **measure**. But many children come to school lacking these "simple" vocabulary concepts. Everyone recognizes that children who come to school with smaller-than-average vocabularies are likely to experience difficulty learning to read and write. These same small vocabularies limit their ability to learn to do math. Explicitly teaching math vocabulary evens the playing field for all children.

This chapter will suggest ways you can incorporate vocabulary instruction as you teach your daily math lesson. When you sharpen your focus on vocabulary during math, your students will be more successful in math and their vocabularies will grow—all with no additional time or resources!

Provide Real, Hands-On Learning for Math Vocabulary

All people learn best when they have real, direct experience with whatever they are learning. Most of the vocabulary learning children do before they come to school is based in real things and real experiences. Children first learn to name things—table, chair, cat, dog, for instance. Two-year-olds delight in pointing to the objects they can see and naming them all. Put them in a new environment, such as the beach or the doctor's office, and they will almost immediately begin to point to things and ask, "What's that?" Nouns are not the only words that children learn through direct experience. Every young child knows the meanings of *run* and *walk* and has probably been told many times that you can't run in the parking lot! Children learn emotion words through real experiences—for example, "I know you feel sad that your friend moved away. I would be sad, too, if that happened to me."

The words we know best and remember longest are those with which we have had real, direct experience. Because effective math instruction emphasizes concrete, hands-on manipulatives, math is the perfect venue for developing vocabulary through real, direct experiences. Unfortunately, the very children whose vocabularies are most limited and who most need these hands-on experiences often attend schools where worksheets and "test prep" absorb most of the instructional time. Teachers and administrators in schools with large numbers of poor children are under such pressure to increase test scores that they may feel they can't devote time to the very experiences that would build the foundation for the success they are trying to achieve. Effective math instruction at all grade levels begins with hands-on manipulative experiences. These same experiences teach the essential vocabulary in a deep and lasting way.

Manipulate Your Students!

When providing real experiences for vocabulary development in mathematics instruction, consider your students as your first and most important manipulatives. Imagine that you wanted to build these vocabulary terms as part of a unit in geometry:

inside   outside   circle   square   triangle   corner   rectangle   sides

How could you use your children as the manipulatives to introduce these concepts? Many teachers have not done this, but when asked to construct an activity to teach these concepts using the children, they very quickly see how that could be done.

> "I would have half the class come to the front of the room and form a circle. They would hold hands, and we would make as big a circle as we could so the circle would be as round as possible. I would then ask some of the students who were not part of the circle to go inside the circle. The remainder of the class would stand outside the circle. I would get all the children to use the words **circle, inside,**

and **outside** by asking questions such as, 'Where is Ceretha?' and 'Where is Carlton?' I would have my class respond chorally in sentences:

Ceretha is inside the circle.
Carlton is outside the circle.

"Next, I would choose 12 children and form them into a square. I would have them stand very close together and make clear corners. We would count the sides and decide that a square has four sides and that the sides are the same length. We would notice and count the corners. I would have children outside the square go inside and outside the square and repeat the procedure. I would ask some of the children inside and outside to stand at the corners. To make a rectangle, I would add two more children to two opposite sides and let my children see that we still have four sides, but the sides to which I added the children got longer. The triangle is simple. I would send the children on one side of the rectangle to their seats and form the remaining children into a shape with three sides and three corners.

"After we had formed the shapes with my directions, I would put children into groups and ask them to form the shapes in their groups. I would continue to have the children use the words to describe the shape they formed, count corners and sides, and ask different children to stand inside or outside the shape."

Using the children as manipulatives can also work when introducing more sophisticated geometry concepts to older children. How would you use your children as the manipulatives to demonstrate the terms **circumference, radius,** and **diameter**? Could you arrange your students into formations to show **right, acute,** and **obtuse** angles?

Mathematical concepts can always be made concrete because mathematics represents the real world. Whenever possible, when introducing new math concepts and terms, consider having your students experience the concepts very concretely by turning them into the manipulatives.

Seek Out Real-World Examples of the Concept

After introducing the concepts by manipulating your students, write the words you introduced on index cards and engage your children in a game of I Spy. Show each index card and have everyone chorally pronounce each word. Remind them of what each word means by reminding them of what they did to represent the word. Next, choose someone to give a clue about something in the room. Begin the game by modeling the types of clues you want them to give:

"I spy some corners on the door."

"I spy someone wearing a pin that is a circle."

"I spy a desk that is a rectangle."

Choose a student to answer the riddle, walk and point to the object, and then come up with the next riddle.

If you taught the terms **right, obtuse,** and **acute** angles by forming your students into these angles, can your students find any of these angles in the objects of your room? As you walk to the cafeteria or out to the playground, are there any right, obtuse, or acute angles? Does your school have a ramp that your students could observe to notice both the acute and obtuse angles formed at the bottom and top? Can your students manipulate their hands into a right angle and then turn it into an obtuse and an acute angle? Could you use pizza—or a pizza model—to teach **circumference, radius,** and **diameter**?

Use Manipulatives and Cut and Fold Paper

In addition to using your students as manipulatives and seeking out examples of the vocabulary terms in your school world, you can provide real experiences with math concepts by using various objects as manipulatives. Could your students arrange popcorn or Cheerios® into circles? Squares? Rectangles? Triangles? Could they place the cup that contained the popcorn or Cheerios® inside and outside the shape? At the corner of the shape?

Could your older students form a right angle with popcorn or Cheerios® and then manipulate it into an acute and obtuse angle? Could they form two circles, one inside the other, that had different circumferences and then place more popcorn or Cheerios® inside the circles to demonstrate the diameter? Could they eat half the popcorn in the circle to turn the diameter into a radius?

Paper folding and cutting is another way to provide concrete experiences for your students with these geometry concepts. How do you fold a square to turn it into a rectangle? A triangle? How do you fold a circle to show the diameter? The radius?

Commercially produced math manipulatives are fine, but if you don't have easy access to them, cereal and popcorn are nutritious alternatives, and children enjoy eating their manipulatives as directed during the activity and at the end to clean up! Providing students with manipulatives to teach concepts does not have to be an expensive and time-consuming activity.

Drawings and Other Visual Representations

In addition to providing a variety of real, concrete experiences with mathematics vocabulary, children can solidify their vocabulary knowledge by creating drawings and other visuals to illustrate the concepts. After working with circles, rectangles, and squares and with the concepts of **inside, outside, sides,** and **corners,** children can create illustrations that show these concepts. Older children could also create illustrations of the concepts **circumference, diameter, radius,** and **right, obtuse,** and **acute angles.** Many teachers have their students record their visual representations in a math notebook or journal. Students are allowed to represent the concepts as directly or imaginatively as they like, with the only requirement being that the vocabulary words be clearly written and correctly linked to the concept.

Other kinds of visual representation that many teachers use in math lessons include various types of charts and graphs based on data collected. In primary grades, teachers create simple bar graphs based on children's favorite colors or birthday months. Once you create these charts, you can

Illustrations Depicting Concepts

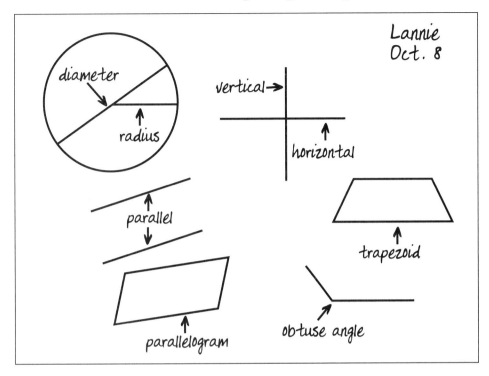

use them to teach children comparative words such as **more, less, greater, most,** and **least**. Older children can strengthen their concepts of **average, mean, mode, median,** and **range** by graphing and labeling data based on probability experiments. Students particularly enjoy showing data in various representations if they can use the spreadsheet technology available on most school computers.

A different kind of visual representation of mathematical terms can be found in a great variety of picture books that illustrate mathematical concepts. Just as there is a wide variety of wonderful alphabet books, there is an abundance of imaginative counting books. Older children are fascinated by big numbers and will enjoy Robert E. Wells's *Is a Blue Whale the Biggest Thing There Is?* and *Can You Count to a Googol?*. David M. Schwartz helps children conceptualize a million—and other enormous numbers in several books, including *If You Made a Million*. David Adler has written several intriguing math books, including *How Tall, How Short, How Far*

Our Birthday Months

December	Josh	Joyce			
November	Ayana	Carlton			
October	Kevin M	Patrice	Jacob		
September	David				
August					
July	Grant	Kathleen			
June	Kevin C	Liz	Roberto		
May	James	Merrill			
April	Terry	Don	Zack	Scott	Ginna
March	Willy				
February	Corina	Matt			
January	Sarah				

Away? Because these books have wonderful illustrations, they are often shelved with the picture books in school and public libraries. Teachers of older children often don't realize that wonderful resources for providing visual experiences to build math concepts are waiting to be discovered just down the hall!

Reading aloud to children daily was recommended in Chapter 2 as one of the most important tools you have for building meaning vocabulary. Include some of the captivating math-related books in your read-aloud, and you can "kill two birds with one stone." Make these books available for children to choose during their independent reading time, and your students who like math will find books they enjoy and, perhaps, learn to like reading better!

Talking and Writing

Chapter 1 included seven principles for effective vocabulary instruction. The activities described so far in this chapter help you put into practice three of these principles:

- Vocabulary is learned best when it is based on real, concrete experiences.
- Pictures and other visuals help solidify word meanings.
- A set of essential words, including academic subject-area vocabulary, should be directly taught.

Incorporating activities such as List, Group, and Label and writing in math journals will help you accomplish another important principle:

- To truly own a word, you must use that word in talking and writing.

List, Group, and Label

A List, Group, and Label lesson for words collected during reading was described in Chapter 3. Here is how you can use this same lesson template to get your students to speak math vocabulary.

Put your students in trios or quartets and give them a list of vocabulary words you have introduced and that you want to become part of their core math vocabulary. You can do this activity with words from just one math topic, but when you have taught several topics, include words from the different topics so children can think about how they are related. This activity works best if your students can actually manipulate the words, so you may want to give them the words in a form that they can cut up into individual words. Here are the math words included when a unit on Patterns and Measurement had been taught:

cent	coin	length	width	ounce
foot	hour	gallon	short	pound
month	dime	quart	inch	yard
same	minute	mile	tall	dollar
sort	quarter	long	size	day
week	classify	different	alike	year

The children in each trio or quartet gather together and quickly cut apart the words on the sheet. The students are told that their job is to find words that go together in some way and put their words together to form a category, or group. Once they have made a group of words, their task is to come up with a name or label for that group. A recorder in each student group writes down the words and their label. Then the children should each take back their words and try to think of another group. The words in the first group can be recycled into the second group if the second group requires the words. Once students have created and labeled a second group, have the recorder record this group and label. If there is time, the students should put all the words back in the pool and form a third or a fourth group.

When the allotted time is up—10 to 15 minutes—let each group of students share one of their word groups and call on volunteers to guess what they labeled it. Here are some of the groups created by students who worked with the list above:

same, different; labeled "opposites"
week, month, year, day; labeled "things on a calendar"
ounce, pound; labeled "things you can weigh"
cent, coin, dime, quarter, dollar; labeled "money"
classify, sort; labeled "things you do with stuff"

A quick extension that really stretches their thinking can be done after the students have shared one of their groups. Give them two minutes to see whether they can come up with other words not included on the list that belong in their group.

List, Group, and Label is a simple but engaging way to get your students to think about important vocabulary and to talk with one another about the attributes of each word. Children enjoy creating the groups and guessing the labels for the groups their classmates make. Thinking of the labels is hard for some children, but it forces them to think about how the words go together, and working as a group, they can usually come up with an appropriate label. If you do List, Group, and Label activities periodically to review math vocabulary and give the students two minutes after they have made and shared their groups to add words to a group, you will find that they begin thinking about words they could add while making the groups.

Math Journals

When you put your students into groups to List, Group, and Label, you get your students talking about the vocabulary. To get them using the words in writing, many teachers incorporate key vocabulary into math journal assignments. Math journals have become popular in recent years as teachers have realized the power of having students summarize what they learn each day in a quick journal entry. Journal entries can include steps for solving various kinds of math problems, real-world examples of the math being studied, and reactions to picture books read aloud that build math concepts and math vocabulary. After being the manipulatives and using their bodies to demonstrate circle, square, rectangle, triangle, inside, outside, corner, and sides, students might be asked to write two true sentences in their journals using at least two of the vocabulary words in each sentence. Have them underline the vocabulary words to be sure they have used at least two. Once they have written two sentences, volunteers can read their sentences, and the other class members can give them a "thumbs up" if the sentence is true. Here are some of the sentences written by students. Notice that while the requirement is for two words per sentence, some students challenge themselves to use as many words as they can.

> You can stand <u>inside</u> and <u>outside</u> the <u>circle</u>.
> <u>Circles</u> don't have <u>sides</u> and <u>corners</u>.
> <u>Rectangles</u> and <u>squares</u> have four <u>sides</u> and four <u>corners</u>.

Triangles have three sides.

Circles don't have sides and corners, but squares, rectangles, and triangles have them, and you can stand inside and outside all of them.

Numbers for English Language Learners

Numbers are the same in almost every language! The words for the numbers are different, but the numerals—1; 13; 1,000; 1,000,000—are the same. Math is a subject many English language learners excel in because they recognize the numbers and can make connections to their first language. Focusing on the vocabulary of math—the specialized words used to talk about math—allows children learning English to be more successful and to learn many essential English words. Doing a variety of vocabulary activities that include real and visual experiences allows your English language learners to learn English vocabulary in the same way that young children learn most of their vocabulary words. Structuring opportunities to use the words in talking and writing provides additional experiences with the words and helps all students—especially students learning English—to develop deep and rich knowledge of the words' meanings and how they are used.

The Vocabulary of Mathematics

Math contains a lot of specialized vocabulary—vocabulary specific to the subject of mathematics. Some terms such as **divisor, rectangle,** and **place value** are commonly used only in mathematics, and children need to learn their meaning. For most children, these words are new words for new concepts. Other terms are used in math and in the non-math world with roughly the same meaning, such as **measure, half,** and **tally.** Because these concepts are part of the non-math world, many children have the concepts, if not the words for these concepts. These vocabulary words are examples of new words for old meanings. Another group of terms includes multimeaning words. **Prime, odd,** and **right** have a common non-mathematical meaning—**prime** rib, **odd** question, **right** answer—and students must learn the new (and often unrelated) meaning. In this case, they are learning new meanings for old words.

Most teachers know that they have to teach the specialized vocabulary of math for children to be successful in math. But many teachers don't realize the potential to increase the general vocabularies of their students while teaching mathematics. In this section, we will think about how you can expand students' non-math vocabulary while teaching vocabulary essential to math.

The Common Core State Standards in Mathematics specify topics that should be the focus of instruction at each grade level. In kindergarten, first, and second grade, the standards relate to operations and algebraic thinking, numbers and operations in base 10, geometry, measurement, and data. Work with whole numbers is emphasized in kindergarten through second grade. Fractions are added as an important topic in third grade, and standards that include both fractions and decimals are included in grades four and five.

For each topic, I have created a list of the most common and essential vocabulary. The list is subdivided according to words needed in grades K through 2 and grades 3 through 5. I compiled this list by consulting the National Council of Teachers of Mathematics standards (NCTM, 2000) and the Common Core State Standards. I also consulted the list of mathematical terms compiled by Robert Marzano and included in the Appendix of *Building Background Knowledge for Academic Achievement* (2004).

The list of basic mathematical terms is included only to show the potential for vocabulary development while teaching mathematics. Given your curriculum, there will be words you will want to add, and there may be some words you will want to delete. The list includes some very common words that are important to mathematics but that may be so well known by your students that they don't deserve any instructional emphasis. The words are arbitrarily assigned to grades K through 2 or 3 through 5, and you will likely find words on one list that in your school belong on the other list. Look at the lists as a starting point for thinking about expanding your students' math and non-math vocabulary during your everyday math instruction.

Vocabulary for Numbers and Operations

For many teachers, this is the part of the mathematics curriculum that is most familiar. Children learn to **count, add, subtract, multiply,** and **divide.** They perform these functions with **whole numbers, decimals,** and **fractions.** The essential vocabulary for this topic includes the following words:

Numbers and Operations, Grades K through 2

add	forwards	number	subtract
addition	group	odd	subtraction
backwards	half	ones	sum
count	hundred	place value	tens
difference	less	plus	total
digit	minus	regroup	whole
equal	more	rename	zero
even	none	set	

Look at the words K–2 children need to use and understand to be successful with numbers and operations. Which words are math words only? Which words have the same meaning in math as they do in general use? Which words are multimeaning words with a different meaning in math from the meaning children might already know? Do any words have word parts that might help children remember what they mean and that might help them learn how these word parts work?

For most K–2 children, the words **add, addition, sum, subtract, subtraction, digit, place value, rename,** and **regroup** are specific math terms. They are taught during math time through concrete experiences as children manipulate objects and learn to add and subtract.

Backwards, forwards, count, group, less, more, whole, half, equal, tens, ones, none, zero, hundred, and **total** are examples of words that have a general use that is very much like the mathematical use. If you teach the general meaning of these words along with the mathematical meaning, you can use the familiar meaning to connect to the mathematical meaning for children who know that meaning and you can teach the general meaning for that word for children who don't know it. To introduce the concept of **forwards**

and **backwards,** for instance, you might let children move cars forwards and backwards and then make the connection to counting forwards and backwards. The concepts of **group, less,** and **more** can be taught in the non-mathematical sense by having students pile up groups of various objects and deciding which group has more and which group has less. The concepts of **whole** and **half** can be developed by having children share something—an apple, a sandwich, or a piece of paper. The concepts of **zero** and **none** can be developed by relating them to a ballgame in which the final score was 5 to 0. How many points did the losing team score? None! Children hear and use the word **hundred** in their real world. Does anyone know someone who is 100 years old? Do they know that a football field is 100 yards? All these words—and many more—have a general meaning and a mathematical meaning that are very similar. By starting with the general meaning, you can quickly help extend a known concept to the world of mathematics. For any children—including English language learners who don't know the general meanings—you are teaching general vocabulary they need to know.

Some words have a general meaning that is quite different from the mathematical meaning. The words **even** and **odd,** for example, are used in phrases such as these:

"I have two, and you have two. Now we're even."

"We got beat, even though we played hard."

"It is odd that he is so late and he didn't call."

"I like Uncle Joe, but he is a little odd."

These meanings of **even** and **odd** show very little resemblance to the math-ematical use of even and odd numbers. When learning multimeaning mathematical vocabulary such as **even, odd, difference,** and **set,** children may be confused by the other meaning of the word they already know. Having children access their familiar meaning of the word first and then explaining that the word has a different meaning in math staves off cognitive confusion and teaches both meanings of the word for those who don't know the more common meaning. Before teaching the term **set** in math, have children think of things that come in sets, such as Legos and tea party dishes. Have children compare objects and describe the difference between them before teaching the mathematical meaning for **difference**.

Many of the key mathematical terms contain familiar word parts. Pointing out these word parts to your students can help you achieve this important goal.

- Students should be taught strategies for learning new words independently from reading, including instruction in word parts, context, and effective use of the dictionary.

Whenever you are teaching a math word that has any common word parts, seize the opportunity to help children learn how these word parts work. For the K–2 Numbers and Operations Vocabulary, you could point out that **rename** and **regroup** start with the prefix **re** and that **re** often means "again." "Robert, when you replay a game, you play it again." "Anna, when you restart the computer, you start it again." **Rename** means "name again" and **regroup** means "group again." Second-graders could think about the relationships between **add/addition** and **subtract/subtraction**. Begin with some **tion** pairs they know, such as **collect/collection** and **direct/direction**. Help them see that what they have when they collect baseball cards is a baseball card collection. "Tony, when you direct someone how to go someplace, you give them directions." "Olivia, when you add, you are doing addition, and when you subtract, you are doing subtraction." You may also want to point out that when your students count backwards, they are counting back. Drawing the children's attention to word parts helps them develop deeper meanings for the vocabulary and reminds them that many big words are made up of familiar word parts.

Numbers and Operations, Grades 3 through 5

associative	division	million	product
billion	divisor	multiples	quotient
commutative	equivalent	multiplication	rational
decimal	estimation	multiply	rounding
denominator	factor	negative	thousand
distributive	fractions	numerator	trillion
divide	improper	percent	
dividend	infinite	prime	

In the upper grades, there is also math vocabulary that is specific to math, vocabulary for which the general meaning and the math meaning are closely related, and multimeaning vocabulary for which the general meaning might mislead students about the math meaning. Many of the math vocabulary words for upper grades have word parts that will help students develop a deeper meaning for the words and that will help students learn to use word parts as meaning clues to new words. From the Numbers and Operations, Grades 3 through 5 list, the following words are probably specific to math terms:

divisor quotient equivalent associative commutative thousand million billion trillion multiples multiply multiplication denominator numerator percent decimal fraction

These words need to be explicitly taught using as many real and visual experiences as you can provide. Because these are both new words and new concepts, students need to have a variety of experiences with these words, including using these words in speaking and writing.

The words **divide, estimation,** and **infinite** are words that have a general meaning and a math meaning that are closely related. Beginning with the general meanings that many of your students know allows you to then help them transfer their knowledge to the specific mathematical meanings.

Words whose general meaning and mathematical meaning are closely connected help students quickly acquire math vocabulary. Some words, however, have a general meaning that is not clearly related to the mathematical meaning, and if students know the general meaning, they could be confused by the math concept. When introducing math words whose general meaning might lead students astray, attack the problem head on by helping students access the general meaning and then explaining that these words have a different mathematical meaning. Here are some general meanings your students may have that will not help them learn these math terms:

dividend—stocks pay dividends
division—the automotive division
factor—many factors in making a decision
improper—improper behavior
prime—prime time

product—anything that is produced
rational—rational thinking
rounding—rounding up cattle

Words with Helpful Parts

This set of words has many words with helpful word parts. You may want students to notice that **multiply, multiples,** and **multiplication** all begin with the prefix **multi,** meaning "many." Other common words in which **multi** means "many" are **multitudes, multinational,** and **multiracial.** The words **divide, dividend, divisor,** and **division** all share the same root. The prefix **im** gives **improper** its opposite meaning, just as it does in **impossible, impatient,** and **imperfect.** The adjectives **associative** and **distributive** have the same root as the verbs **associate** and **distribute** and the nouns **association** and **distribution.**

Math Cognates for English Language Learners

Many of the mathematical terms your students need to learn have Spanish cognates. If you teach children who speak Spanish, be alert for these cognates. Here are some cognates for common math terms:

English Word	Spanish Word
area	área
center	centro
circle	circulo
congruent	congruente
cylinder	cilindro
distance	distancia
dollar	dolór
estimate	estimar
gallon	galón
hour	hora

English Word	Spanish Word
milligram	miligramo
million	millón
minute	minuto
negative	negativo
parallel	paralelo
quarter	cuarto
zero	cero

Math Vocabulary for Geometry, Measurement, Algebra, and Data

Here are the lists of common mathematical terms for the other four math topics. Just as for Numbers and Operations, use these lists as starting points for developing your list of core math vocabulary for these topics. Think about which words are specific to math and need to be taught with concrete, hands-on experiences. For which words do your students have a general meaning that will help them quickly develop the mathematical meaning? Which words are multimeaning words with a general meaning that is quite different from the mathematical meaning and that might confuse students and interfere with their understanding of the mathematical meaning? Introduce these multimeaning words by reminding students of the general meaning and explicitly teaching them that these words have different meanings in mathematics. Many words in all four topics have word parts that will help students solidify the meaning of the word and expand their vocabularies.

Geometry (K–2)

above	circle	long	short
after	cone	middle	sides
before	corner	outside	square
behind	cube	over	tall
below	direction	rectangle	top
between	inside	right	triangle
bottom	left	shape	under

Geometry (3–5)

acute	flip	plane	rotation
angle	horizontal	polygon	segment
axis	intersect	prism	slide
circumference	isosceles	pyramid	solid
congruent	obtuse	radius	sphere
cylinder	parallel	ray	symmetric
diagonal	parallelogram	reflection	transformation
diameter	pentagon	rhombus	trapezoid
equilateral	perpendicular	right (angle)	vertical

Measurement (K–2)

calendar	gallon	money	time
cent	greater	month	volume
clock	height	most	week
coin	high	nickel	weigh
compare	hour	ounce	weight
cup	inch	penny	wide
dime	least	pint	width
distance	length	pound	yard
dollar	long	quart	year
estimate	measure	quarter	
fewer	mile	seconds	
foot	minutes	temperature	

Measurement (3–5)

area	Fahrenheit	meter	perimeter
capacity	gram	metric	thermometer
Celsius	kilometer	milligram	
centimeter	liter	milliliter	
degrees	mass	millimeter	

Algebra and Patterns (K–2)

alike	first	properties	size
classify	order	same	sort
different	pattern	second	third

Algebra and Patterns (3–5)

array	diagram	inequality	proof
bar graph	equation	line graph	variable
constant	function	pie graph	

Data Analysis and Probability (K–2)

chance	graph	outcome	table
collect	organize	predict	tally

Data Analysis and Probability (3–5)

average	grid	midpoint	probability
data	mean	mode	range
function	median	model	ratio

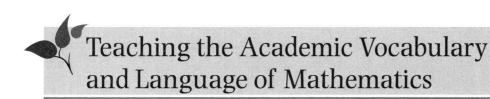

Teaching the Academic Vocabulary and Language of Mathematics

In his powerful book, *Building Background Knowledge for Academic Achievement,* Robert Marzano (2004) makes the case for the direct teaching of vocabulary in every subject area. He refers to content-specific words as "academic vocabulary" and argues that the enormous task of providing direct and explicit teaching of anything close to the 1,000 to 3,000 words students need to add to their vocabularies each year becomes much more reasonable if vocabulary instruction is part of every subject area every day. Furthermore, in addition to maximizing the number of words it is possible to teach well, teaching the academic vocabulary of a subject area maximizes the potential for learning in that subject area. Elementary teachers spend approximately an hour each day teaching mathematics. Across the K–5 years, that hour each day adds up to over 1,000 hours of math instruction. If just a fraction of that 1,000 hours was devoted to engaging vocabulary instruction, all children would leave elementary school with larger vocabularies and stronger mathematical concepts.

chapter 9

Building Vocabulary While You Teach Science

Science is another subject in the elementary curriculum that provides many opportunities

for vocabulary development. Just as in math, children who become fluent with the language of science learn more science while simultaneously expanding their science and general vocabularies. Also like math, effective science instruction includes many hands-on experiments and investigations that provide students with real, concrete experiences that provide anchors for their vocabulary knowledge. To maximize vocabulary development during science, we build on these concrete experiences, provide virtual experiences when real experiences are not possible, and use a variety of pictures and other graphic representations. Because science topics are usually pursued across several weeks of instruction, the variety and repetition required to add new vocabulary words will occur within the learning cycle as key vocabulary is used in various ways.

Just as for math, I compiled a list of core science vocabulary. In constructing the list, I consulted several sources, including Marzano's (2004) list of elementary science vocabulary, *National Science Education Standards* published by the National Research Council (1996), and the elementary science standards for several states. My hope is that teachers view these lists as starting points for developing their own lists. Depending on at what grade level the topic is taught in your curriculum, some words may be too advanced for your students and some words may be so well known that they don't deserve any attention. If your science curriculum includes other topics not included in this list, you can develop your own list of core science vocabulary for that topic.

Provide Real, Hands-On Learning for Science Vocabulary

Experiments and investigations that engage students in real, hands-on learning need to be a part of the learning cycle for every science topic. As an example of how to maximize the potential of this concrete experience for vocabulary development, I have chosen the topic of Electricity and Magnets. Here is the list of core vocabulary I compiled for that topic. (Remember that given your grade level, curriculum, and students, you may want to add or delete words from this list.)

Electricity and Magnets

electricity	insulator	bulb	current
magnets	conductor	wire	charge
attraction	circuit	battery	static
repulsion	parallel	switch	grounded
power	series	generator	

Looking at this list of core vocabulary, it becomes immediately obvious how the hands-on experiments—testing objects to see whether they are attracted or repulsed by magnets, making a light bulb light, constructing a parallel and series circuit, and other experiments—provide the concrete experiences to anchor the development of this vocabulary. Because students will be conducting these experiments in small groups, they will be talking to each other and using the vocabulary words in their discussions. Writing can occur in an uncontrived manner as children write down their predictions of which objects will be attracted to a magnet before experimenting and record their observations after experimenting. For this topic, it seems natural to have students draw and label with the appropriate words the results of some of their experiments.

Drawing and Labeling
the Results of a Science Experiment

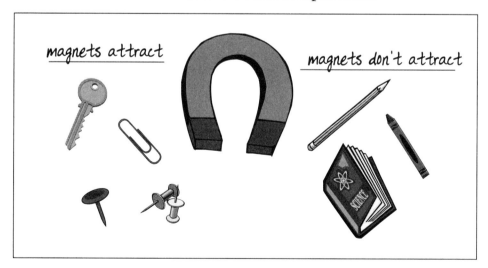

Learn Science Vocabulary through Virtual Fieldtrips

Although hands-on experiences are the most powerful vocabulary anchors, not all science topics can be experienced in a hands-on manner. Consider how you would anchor vocabulary for these core words in a unit on the Solar System.

Solar System

solar system	Mars	eclipse	gravity
astronomy	Jupiter	rotation	shadow
sky	Venus	orbit	comet
sun	Neptune	planet	meteor
star	Mercury	revolve	asteroid
constellation	Saturn	outer space	galaxy
moon	Uranus	telescope	
Earth	universe	atmosphere	

A few of these concepts could be developed concretely. You could have your students conduct an experiment using a flashlight and a globe and demonstrate **revolve** and **shadows**. Most of these concepts, however, cannot be demonstrated or simulated in a classroom. This is when you are glad to be teaching in the digital age, and you make plans to take your students on some virtual fieldtrips. Both the NASA website (www.nasa.gov/forkids) and the Smithsonian Art and Space website (www.nasm.si.edu) provide a huge variety of virtual exploration possibilities. Captivating videos and animations are available at Solarviews (www.solarviews.com).

The much-loved Ms. Frizzle is the "Mother of Virtual Fieldtrips." Don't miss the opportunity to read *The Magic School Bus Lost in the Solar System* by Joanna Cole to your students as part of the unit. Other Magic School Bus science books include *The Magic School Bus Plants Seeds, The Magic School Bus Inside the Human Body, The Magic School Bus on the Ocean Floor,* and *The Magic School Bus Inside the Earth.*

Use Pictures and Other Visuals

Your virtual fieldtrips will, of course, include videos and other pictures. You can also use the pictures in science books to build vocabulary. Look back at the Picture Walk example in Chapter 7 in which students used pictures to build meanings for important words before reading about volcanoes and about animals and their habitats. In Chapter 5, pictures were included along with context and word parts as important clues students could use to independently sleuth out the meaning of words. The Preview-Predict-Confirm lesson described in Chapter 5 in which students predicted which words would occur in a book about penguins after viewing visuals from the book can be used to introduce science vocabulary for any text that has a lot of visuals. Word Detectives, another lesson template used to teach students to figure out meanings of words independently, had students working in trios and using the text to figure out the meanings of these six words.

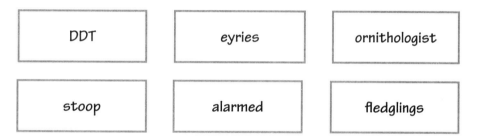

Including Picture Walks, PPC lessons, and Word Detective activities to introduce science vocabulary will help your students transfer their strategies for independent vocabulary acquisition to the language of science.

Include Science Books in Teacher Read-aloud and Independent Reading

Many key concepts and vocabulary for science topics can easily be developed through hands-on experiments, but there are some concepts that children cannot experience directly. Animals, for example, is a popular science topic with children, and there are many beautifully written and illustrated books about animals. Gail Gibbons, the most prolific writer of informational books about animals, has dozens of titles, including *Dogs, Sharks, Penguins,* and *Horses.* Many teachers share one or two of Gail Gibbons's animal books with the whole class. Next, they form the class into groups to read her books and books by other authors about animals of their choosing.

Children can extend their knowledge of any science topic and vocabulary if you choose books like these for your teacher read-aloud and make them available to your students during their independent reading time.

- The Let's-Read-and-Find-Out Science series (HarperCollins) includes almost 100 titles such as *Energy Makes Things Happen; Switch On, Switch Off; Floating in Space;* and *What's It Like to Be a Fish?*

- The Rookie Read-About Science series (Scholastic) includes dozens of books including *What Is Friction?; It Could Still Be a Robot;* and *What Is Electricity?*

- The Windows on Literacy Science Focus series (National Geographic) includes hundreds of titles for young readers including *A Frog Has a Sticky Tongue, Simple Machines,* and *Magnets.*

- For older students, the Reading Expeditions Science series (National Geographic) includes titles such as *Looking at Cells,* and *Matter, Matter Everywhere.*

Encourage Students to Talk and Write Science Words

Remember that to truly own a word, you not only have to hear and read that word but you have to use that word in talking and writing. Chapters 3 and 4 provided suggestions for productive talk and quick-writes. Look back at Chapter 3 and consider opportunities during your science instruction to have students "turn and talk" or participate in quick Think-Pair-Share activities. Science also provides many opportunities for children to participate in structured discussions. Here are a few examples of structured discussions you can use to have your students speak the science vocabulary.

How Do These Go Together?

Give students a list of the key vocabulary you have been working on. Put students in trios and give each trio three or four index cards. Tell them that you want them to choose two words that go together in some way. On the front of the index card, they should write the two words into this sentence:

_____ and _____ go together because

On the back, they finish the sentence by writing the reason they think these words go together.

Give the trios 9–10 minutes to complete a few index cards and then gather the class together. Let each trio share one of their sentences. Have them read the sentence beginning they wrote on the front of the card and call on members of other trios to guess the answer they wrote on the back. Be sure to acknowledge that there might be other good reasons for words to go together besides the reason written on the back of the card. Here are the cards some children made using vocabulary words from a unit on the Solar System.

Cards for How Do These Go Together? Activity

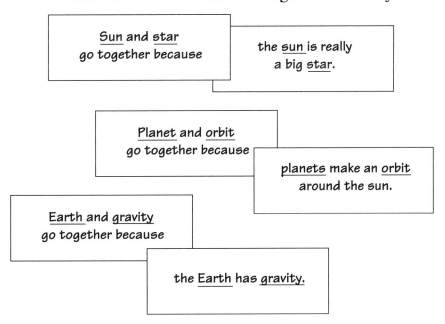

Sun and star
go together because

the sun is really
a big star.

Planet and orbit
go together because

planets make an orbit
around the sun.

Earth and gravity
go together because

the Earth has gravity.

Fill in My Blank

Have students work together to write a sentence using one of the words. Tell them to write the sentence and underline the vocabulary word. Ask students to read the sentence aloud and have other students guess the word that goes in the blank. Students will often use more than one vocabulary word in the sentence, but they should choose just one blank for others to guess. Some sentences will follow closely the context in which students learned them, and others will use the words in different contexts. Accept whatever sentences students come up with as long as the sentences make sense. Here are some sentences students constructed using the Solar System vocabulary.

> <u>Uranus</u> is the seventh planet from the sun.
> Earth and Saturn are the only planets with an <u>atmosphere</u>.
> One year on <u>Mars</u> is about two Earth years.

Data Charts

Many science topics include comparing and contrasting the different things being studied. Children learn the different characteristics of reptiles, amphibians, mammals, fish, birds, and insects. They compare igneous, metamorphic, and sedimentary rocks. A more extended structured discussion activity can be created by having trios of students complete a data chart summarizing the characteristics of each member of the group. The core vocabulary for the Solar System includes the names of the eight planets in the solar system of Earth. To get students talking about the planets and the features of the planets, put your students to work in groups and have them complete a data chart summarizing the most important information about these planets. It is important that you have

The Planets

Planet	Size	Distance from Sun	Atmosphere	Weather	Year	Special
Earth	Medium	Third	Nitrogen and oxygen	Moderate	365 days	Plants, animals, and people
Venus	Almost same as Earth	Second	Carbon dioxide	Hot	225 Earth days	Rotates opposite direction
Mercury	Smallest	Closest	Almost none	Hot-day Cold-night	88 Earth days	Iron core
Mars	Almost same as Earth	Fourth	Carbon dioxide	Cold	2 Earth years	Huge canyon
Uranus	Third largest	Seventh	Hydrogen and helium	Cold	84 Earth years	10 rings 15 moons
Saturn	Second largest	Sixth	Hydrogen	Cold, windy	30 Earth years	Rings made of rocks, ice, and dust
Neptune	Same as Uranus	Farthest	Hydrogen and helium	Cold, windy	165 Earth years	Visited by Voyager 2
Jupiter	Largest	Fifth	Hydrogen and helium	Cold	12 Earth years	Mostly made of gases

them complete this chart as a group because your real purpose is for them to use Solar System vocabulary as they talk to one another. Completing this chart alone would not accomplish the "talk" purpose. Encourage them to use books and other resources to find information. Once they complete the data chart as a group, have each child choose one planet and do a quick-write in which they write a paragraph summarizing the information on the chart.

The planet Earth holds its atmosphere because of gravity.
Venus is about the same size as Earth.

In this example, the class was studying animals, and students were learning this important science vocabulary.

Animals Core Vocabulary
(Include names of animals common to children's environment,
such as dogs, ants, squirrels, bees, fish, etc.)

habitats	amphibians	behaviors	hibernate
birds	reptiles	features	animal
insects	fish	food	
mammals	body parts	shelter	

At the end of the unit, they worked in trios to complete an animal data chart. Notice how students would be using almost all the core animal vocabulary as they talked together about what should go in each box in the data chart.

Animal	Type (insect/ mammal, etc.)	Habitat	Shelter	Food	Body	Behaviors

When the chart was completed, the teacher reminded them of the cinquain poem format they had learned, and students used the information from the chart to write cinquains about the different classes of animals.

Reptiles

Cold   blooded

Snakes,   turtles,   alligators

Bodies   covered   with   scales

Reptiles

Concept Charts

Creating concept charts (Frayer, Frederick, & Klausmeier, 1969) is a way for students to solidify their knowledge of a big concept. To complete this chart, students work together to come up with characteristics, examples, and non-examples. Once they have filled in characteristics, examples, and non-examples, they create their own definition. Part of developing a complete meaning for a word is knowing what it is as well as what it is not. Thinking of non-examples helps students clarify and deepen the concept.

Mammals Concept Chart

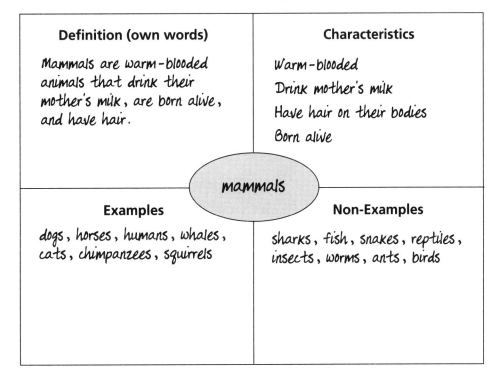

Definition (own words)	Characteristics
Mammals are warm-blooded animals that drink their mother's milk, are born alive, and have hair.	Warm-blooded Drink mother's milk Have hair on their bodies Born alive

mammals

Examples	Non-Examples
dogs, horses, humans, whales, cats, chimpanzees, squirrels	sharks, fish, snakes, reptiles, insects, worms, ants, birds

Science Journals

In many classrooms, students have a special notebook in which they record predictions, observations, and interesting science facts. Back pages of the journal can be used for creating a personal science dictionary. Near the end of a science unit, students consolidate their knowledge of key terms by creating a personal definition and illustration for some of the core vocabulary words.

English Language Learners Need Safe Opportunities to Talk and Write

Think about your own experiences learning a new language. How did you feel when you were called on to speak that language in front of the whole class? Did any of your foreign language instructors put you in small groups and structure activities for you to talk using the new language you were learning? To learn new vocabulary, students must use that vocabulary in talking and writing—but trying out new vocabulary in front of the whole class is an unpleasant and anxiety-producing experience for most people. Having children complete activities with partners and in small groups provides a comfortable environment for speaking the new vocabulary. Be sure to partner or group your English language learners with English-first children who will encourage them and applaud their efforts.

Science Vocabulary Contains Useful Word Parts

Whenever you teach vocabulary in any subject area, ask yourself whether there are other words that you could quickly teach your students by pointing out familiar word parts and talking about how the words are related. Here are just a few of the "bonus words" you could add to your students' vocabularies based on Weather, Solar System, and Animals core words. As you look at the core vocabulary lists, think about all the other words your students could quickly learn.

Science Word	Bonus Words
cloud	cloudy, cloudless
rain	rainy, raincoat, rainstorm
sun	sunny, sunshine, sunflower

Science Word	Bonus Words
snow	snowy, snowstorm
wind	windy, windless
frost	frosty, defrost
freeze	freezer, refreeze, antifreeze, froze, frozen
fog	foggy
evaporation	evaporate
storm	stormy, hailstorm, rainstorm, snowstorm
humidity	humid
pressure	press, impress, depress, compress, pressurize
thermometer	speedometer, barometer, kilometer
meteorologist	meteor, meteorology
habitat	inhabitants
amphibians	amphibious
behavior	behave
hibernate	hibernation
astronomy	astronomer, astronomical, asteroid
universe	universal
rotation	rotate
planet	planetarium, aquarium, terrarium
revolve	revolution
telescope	telescopic, microscopic
atmosphere	atmospheric

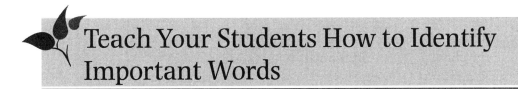

Teach Your Students How to Identify Important Words

It is important that teachers determine what the key vocabulary for a science topic is, but it is equally important that your students learn to do this. Many children, even older children, have difficulty determining what the most important words in a selection are, and thus they have difficulty determining the main ideas. Ten Important Words (Yopp & Yopp, 2007) is a lesson framework you can use to help your students learn to determine which words in an informational text are the most important ones. When your students have chosen the most important words, they have simultaneously identified most of the major concepts or main ideas.

When doing a Ten Important Words lesson, you should not introduce any key vocabulary to students before they read. Rather, you want your students, working in small groups, to choose the key words and decide what these words mean. Begin the lesson by arranging your students into groups of three or four, making sure to include a range of abilities in each group. Give each group 10 small sticky notes and tell them that their job is to read the text together and place the sticky notes on what they think are the most important words. The piece they are reading should be relatively short, three or four pages of a textbook chapter or a two-page spread in a *Weekly Reader, Scholastic News,* or *Time for Kids* magazine. In this example, they are reading a *Time for Kids* article on sea turtles.

As they read, if the students decide other words are more important than the ones they have already designated with sticky notes, they may move the notes around. When the reading time is almost up, stop them and tell them that they must now make their final decisions and write these 10 words—one to a sticky note.

Once the trios have made their choices, gather the students together and create a class tally. Ask each trio to tell you one of their 10 words and then have the other trios show you how many of them also included this word. Write that word and the number of trios that chose it on your list and then ask a second trio for one of their words and get a count of the number of trios that included that word. Continue going around to the different trios until all the words included by any trio are tallied. Here is the tally completed in one classroom after the class had read a selection on sea turtles. This class of 25 students was divided into seven trios and one quartet, so the largest number of votes a word could get was eight. When all the children have read the selection and chosen their 10 words, you make a class tally. For each word chosen by any student or group, tally how many other groups chose that word. The 10 words chosen by the most students become the 10 most important words for that selection and are listed in the order of the number of times the words were chosen. Here are the words chosen by any of the groups and the number of groups that selected that word.

sea turtles	⊢⊢⊢⊢ | | |	8
ocean	⊢⊢⊢⊢ | |	7
eggs	| | |	3
migrate	⊢⊢⊢⊢ | | |	8
endangered	⊢⊢⊢⊢ | |	7
shells	⊢⊢⊢⊢ |	6
flippers	⊢⊢⊢⊢	5
hatch	| | |	3
huge	| | |	3
swimmers	⊢⊢⊢⊢ |	6
nests	⊢⊢⊢⊢ |	6
reptiles	⊢⊢⊢⊢	5
scaly	⊢⊢⊢⊢	5
old	| |	2
jellyfish	| |	2
incubation	|	1

Because they were not in the top 10, the words *eggs, hatch, huge, old, jellyfish,* and *incubation* were eliminated, leaving this list of Top Ten Sea Turtle Words.

1. sea turtles
2. ocean
3. migrate
4. endangered
5. shells
6. flippers

7. swimmers
8. nests
9. reptiles
10. scaly

Once the class tally is established, you can add a quick-write to this lesson by having each student write two sentences, each of which must contain at least two of the top 10 words. Here are a few of the sentences written by students in this class. Notice how writing sentences with key words helps students summarize important information.

Sea turtles are reptiles.

Sea turtles have flippers and are very good swimmers.

Sea turtles live in all the oceans except the Arctic Ocean, which is too cold.

Sea turtles are reptiles with scaly skin.

Sea turtles lay their eggs in nests on the beach.

Sea turtles are endangered and might be extinct like the dinosaurs.

Most children are not very good at determining the most important words in an information piece. Often, they choose words that are most interesting to them, but not necessarily the most important. If you regularly use the Ten Important Words lesson framework, your students will develop the ability to determine important words as they see which words make the class's final cut for the top 10. Having individual students write one or more sentences using at least two of the important words helps them learn to summarize important textual information.

1. Form groups of three or four students, including some good and struggling readers in each group.
2. Give each group 10 sticky notes and ask them to read the informational piece and decide what they think are the 10 most important words. They should put sticky notes on candidates as they read.
3. When they finish reading, they should move the sticky notes to reflect their consensus about which 10 are most important. When they have agreed on their trio's top 10, they should write their words on the sticky notes.

4. Create a class tally by letting each group share one of their 10 words and having the other groups indicate whether they also had that word. Continue the tally until all possibilities are included in the list.

5. Use the tally to create the class top 10 list.

6. Have each of your students write one or more sentences using at least two of the top 10 words.

WordSift and Wordle—Internet Vocabulary Tools for English Language Learners

The Internet offers you two important tools to help your students build academic vocabulary. Wordle (www.wordle.net) is a free Web application that allows you to create a word cloud based on the frequency of words in a text. It can be used to stimulate students' thinking about the meaning, importance, and relationship of words. WordSift (www.wordsift.com) is another free word cloud tool available on the Internet. Like Wordle, a word cloud is created based on text that is cut and pasted into the application. WordSift also offers important learning supports. Each word can be clicked on to show a collection of related images, a word map, and a listing of sentences from the text that present the word in different contexts. WordSift also sorts words by difficulty and identifies academic words. Both Wordle and WordSift support several different languages, making them particularly helpful to ELLs.

Core Vocabulary for Other Common Science Topics

Here is the core vocabulary for other common science topics. Think about the kinds of real, virtual, visual, talking, and writing experiences in which you could engage your students for maximum science learning and vocabulary development.

Weather

weather	clouds	freezing	hurricane
seasons	hot	sleet	tornado
climate	rain	hail	storm
fall	sun	ice	humidity
winter	snow	fog	high
spring	wind	precipitation	low
summer	warm	evaporation	pressure
thermometer	cool	rain gauge	barometer
temperature	cold	thunder	meteorologist
air	frost	lightning	

Plants

(Include names of plants common to children's environment, such as oak tree, grass, rose bush, hedge, etc.)

plant	leaves	seeds	air
parts	stem	needs	water
roots	flowers	light	soil

Sound

sound	vibration	music	eardrum
wave	pitch	instruments	echo
volume	high	voice	
loud	low	vocal cords	
soft	noise	microphone	

Properties of Substances/Five Senses

substances	freeze	hardness	see
senses	melt	odor	hear
solid	size	float	smell
liquid	shape	sink	taste
gas	color	solution	touch
dissolve	texture	mixture	

Animal and Plant Life Cycles/Adaptation

life cycles	metamorphosis	survival	interaction
adaptation	genetic	prey	species
egg	endangered	predator	cell
larva	extinct	diversity	organism
pupa	parent	habitat	photosynthesis
adult	offspring	prehistoric	
behavior	growth	dinosaurs	

Soil, Rocks, and Minerals

soil	clay	fossils	pebbles
rocks	silt	sedimentary	boulders
minerals	gravel	metamorphic	
sand	humus	igneous	

Ecosystems/Environment

ecosystem	environment	atmosphere	conditions
community	renewable	conservation	recycle
nonliving	nonrenewable	natural	population
pollution	fuel	resources	ozone
decompose	threatened	changes	global warming

Earth and Land Forms

crust	geological	eruption	canyon
mantle	weathering	earthquake	desert
core	landslide	glacier	ocean
erosion	flood	avalanche	formation
deposition	volcano	mountain	

Light and Energy

energy	acceleration	nuclear	forms
light	friction	solar	refraction
force	speed	radiation	reflection
inertia	mass	contract	absorption
momentum	heat	expand	

Motion and Balance

motion	gravity	pulleys	pushing
balance	machines	levers	pulling

Human Body/Nutrition/Health/Safety

body	blood	carbohydrates	doctor
nutrition	respiration	fats	physician
health	oxygen	proteins	poison
safety	digestion	symptoms	medicine
food	circulation	disease	hospital
skeleton	nutrients	infection	emergency
bones	vitamins	germs	accident
muscles	calories	virus	injury
joints	exercise	fever	
heart	weight	nurse	

General Science Terms

The following terms include words for which all elementary-grade students must develop deep and full meanings. Students will have direct experiences with these words because they will do them—**describe, predict, compare**—and they will compile them—**properties, characteristics, features**. Most of these words have a general meaning that is very similar to the science meaning. A few words have a general meaning that is quite different from the science meaning, which might be confusing in the science context.

These words are so commonly used that some teachers might assume students know what these words mean and make the mistake of using these words without any explanation. Many students, however, do not have rich concepts for these words. You can increase their success in science and build their general vocabularies by taking a few minutes to introduce each word and help students connect the word to what they know. Many of these words have related words that share the same root. Teaching the related words helps students build fuller meanings for the target words and helps them learn to use word parts to figure out pronunciations and meanings for new words. Here are some possible general and word part connections for these important science terms.

science/scientist (ciencia/cientifico)   A person who does science is a scientist. We are all scientists in this room when we do science. What does an artist do? A psychologist? A tourist? An organist?

investigation (investigación)   In science, we do investigations to find out things. Detectives and firefighters do investigations to solve crimes and figure out what caused a fire. When we do an investigation, we say we are investigating, and the people doing the investigating are called investigators.

properties   In science, properties are the things we notice about something. Is it hard or soft? Heavy or light? Does it sink or float? These are all properties. There is another meaning of property you may know. We call the things that belong to a person that person's property. Your bike and book bag and video games are your property—they belong to you. The properties you observe in science about an object are that object's property—they belong to the object.

characteristics (caracteristico)   Characteristics are like properties, but we often use the term *characteristics* when we are talking about people or animals. When we read a story, the people in the story are the characters.

observe (observer)   In science, we use all our senses to observe things and figure out their properties. We call what we observe our observations and the people doing the observing are the observers.

predict (predecir)   We predict in reading when we make a guess about what is going to happen in a story. We predict in science when we make a guess about what we will find out before we do an experiment. We call what we predict our predictions. If something is easy to predict, we say it is predictable. Some things—like the weather—are quite unpredictable.

describe (describer)   When we describe something, we tell what it is like— we tell its properties. If we see someone drive away after an accident, we describe the car and the people in the car to the person investigating the accident. We call what we describe a description. Sometimes, we experience something so strange that we can't describe it and we say it is indescribable.

compare (comparer)   We compare things and people every day. We compare ourselves to our brother when we say we are older than our brother. We compare the weather when we say it is hotter today than it was yesterday. We compare the pizzas at two different restaurants and decide which one we like better. When we compare, we make a comparison.

classify   We classify things when we put them into groups according to certain characteristics or properties. Our class is a group that has been put together because you are all in the same grade. When we classify things, we call this their classification. Sometimes our government has put some information together that they don't want everyone to know. This information is kept secret and is called classified. When the information no longer needs to be secret, it is declassified so that everyone can read it.

record   In science, we record our observations and predictions. We record them by writing them down or making a drawing. We record information so we can save it and look at it later. Music is recorded when it is put on a CD. If you miss your favorite TV program, you can record it to watch it later. We call the person or thing that does the recording the recorder.

collect (collector)   When you collect things, such as baseball cards or stamps, you put them together and call them a collection. In science, we collect information about what we are studying.

data (datos)   Data is information that we observe and record. We store information on our computers in data files.

analyze   When we analyze something, we think about what it means. When we read a story, we analyze what the characters do and say to figure out what they are thinking and what they might do next. In science, we analyze our data and try to figure out what it means and predict what might happen next. When we analyze things, we call this our analysis.

communicate (comunicar)   We communicate when we share ideas with others. We communicate by speaking, writing, and drawing. Often, we use the phone or Internet to communicate. In science, we communicate when we share our observations, predictions, and analysis with others. When we communicate, we call this communication.

measure (mensurar)   We measure all kinds of things. Measuring things in science is one way we observe and collect data. We call the results our measurements. Some things cannot be measured. We say they are immeasurable.

graph (gráfica)   Graphs are special kinds of pictures we make in math and science to record and show our data.

diagram (diagrama)   Diagrams help us see how things are connected. In science, we make diagrams to show the life cycle of a frog or how electricity gets to our house.

experiment (experiment)   We do experiments in science to find things out. We change things and observe what happens. Drug companies do experiments with all their medicines before they put them on the market. When something has not yet been proven effective, we say it is experimental.

results (resulta)   Results are how things turn out. We read the newspaper or watch TV in the morning to see the results of last night's ballgame. In science, results are what we have when we finish an experiment.

similarities   Similarities are how things are alike. When two things are similar, they are not exactly the same, but they are very much alike. We look for similarities when we compare things.

differences (differencia)   Differences are the opposite of similarities. We compare things by seeing how they are alike and how they are different. In math, we use the term *difference* to mean the answer we get when we subtract one number from another number.

variables   Variables are things that change or vary. When you are deciding which new shoes to buy, you think about all the variables, including style, brand, color, and cost. In science, variables are things we can change in an experiment. How much light and how much water we give plants are variables. When things are different, we say they vary. What we wear each day to school varies with the weather.

microscope (microscopia)   Scientists use microscopes to look at very tiny things. When something is too small to see without a microscope, we say it is microscopic. Scientists use telescopes to view stars and other things that are very far away. The telescopes have telescopic lenses.

For English Language Learners—Science Cognates in Spanish

Look at all the general science vocabulary words that have Spanish cognates (in parentheses after the English terms). If you have students who speak Spanish, be sure to point out cognates that will help them connect meanings for the English words!

Teaching the Academic Vocabulary of Science

Look again at all the core science vocabulary included in the lists in this chapter. Where are your students going to learn these words if they don't learn them during your science instruction? A few of these words—**weather, electricity, rain**—occur in the everyday language of all your students. Other words—**thermometer, magnet, reptiles**—occur in the everyday language of some children. Many of these words—**friction, precipitation, mammals**—seldom occur in everyday language. Think about the television programs your students watch and the movies and DVDs they see. Think about the books they choose to read. The term **academic vocabulary** is the perfect label for the concept of vocabulary encountered only in the academic world of schools. To be successful, children must expand their vocabulary beyond the words they will encounter in their everyday world. Teaching the academic vocabulary of science, the language of science, will result in gains in science learning and in the size and depth of your students' vocabularies.

chapter 10

Building Vocabulary While You Teach Social Studies

Social studies is an area of the elementary curriculum in which a huge amount of academic vocabulary resides. In addition to general words—such as **community, continent,**

and **democracy**—students need to learn a large number of people and place names—for example, **Abraham Lincoln, Africa,** and **Pacific Ocean**. Just as in science, many children learn some of the social studies core vocabulary in everyday conversations, but most words occur only as children engage in learning about the history, geography, cultures, economy, and politics of the world they inhabit.

Constructing the lists of core social studies vocabulary was the most challenging task this book presented because social studies instruction is basically teaching "the world"! Believing, however, that teachers are more apt to emphasize vocabulary if they have a list of important words for which all their students need to develop rich meanings, I developed this list, which I hope will launch teachers into developing their own core social studies vocabulary. To develop the list, I consulted Marzano's (2004) terms for General History, U.S. History, Geography, Civics, and Economics. I also consulted the *Expectations of Excellence: Curriculum Standards for Social Studies* (NCSS, 1994) and the social studies standards of several different states. All the lists are presented here. The remainder of the chapter suggests vocabulary strategies and activities that seem to work best in social studies.

Social Studies Vocabulary

Families/Neighborhoods/Communities

aunt	family	mayor	similarities
brother	future	neighborhood	sister
celebrations	generation	parents	suburban
change	grandparents	past	town
city	group	police	traditions
community	grow	present	uncle
cousin	holidays	relatives	urban
customs	individuals	rituals	
differences	leaders	rural	

Citizenship

citizen	fairness	liberty	rights
citizenship	honesty	patriotism	rules
courage	integrity	pledge	sharing
determination	justice	prejudice	truth
discrimination	laws	respect	
diversity	leaders	responsibility	

Geography
(Plus names of countries and cultures being studied)

border	environment	midwest	scale
climate	forest	mountains	south
coast	geography	north	South Pole
compass	globe	North Pole	southeast
continent	grid	northeast	southwest
country	island	ocean	valley
desert	lake	peninsula	wetlands
direction	latitude	plains	west
distance	location	plateau	world
earth	longitude	region	
east	map	river	

Economics

advertising	employee	needs	spending
allowance	employer	poverty	stores
banks	export	producer	surplus
business	goods	products	taxes
buyer	import	profits	trade
competition	income	resources	training
consumer	interdependence	revenue	transportation
cost	investment	salary	unemployment
customer	job	savings	wages
debt	labor	scarcity	wants
earn	manufacturing	seller	workers
economy	money	services	

State History/Geography
(Plus important people and place names for your state)

agriculture	economy	local	state
capital	governor	population	tourism
cities	history	recreation	towns
counties	industry	region	transportation

U.S. History
(Plus important people and place names)

abolition	depression	integration	reconstruction
amendments	election	inventions	representatives
America	emancipation	judicial	reservation
assassination	equality	legislature	revolution
campaign	executive	majority	segregation
civil war	explorer	minority	senators
colonist	freedom	nation	settlers
colony	frontier	patriot	slavery
confederacy	government	pilgrims	taxes
constitution	immigrants	pioneers	union
country	independence	president	United States
democracy	Indians	railroads	vote

Building Vocabulary through Real Experiences

The most striking difference between the social studies vocabulary lists and the math and science lists is the large number of words for which real, hands-on experiences cannot be provided. Social studies vocabulary is replete with abstract concepts—**citizenship, democracy,** and **segregation.** Even the words that are real things—**continents, plains, mountains,** and **oceans**—are not readily available to most teachers and students. Many social studies terms—such as **pilgrims, colonists,** and **pioneers**—existed at a prior time in history but are no longer part of our everyday experience.

The fact that many social studies concepts are not easily taught through direct experience does not change the fact that new concepts and the vocabulary words that describe those concepts are best learned through real experience. Knowing that children need direct experiences to truly own words, many teachers introduce social studies words to children using simulations and fieldtrips.

You may not think you use simulations in your teaching of social studies, but you probably do. Think of the Thanksgiving feasts primary teachers often invite parents to. Children learn about the first Thanksgiving and dress up as pilgrims or Indians to celebrate the feast. In addition to learning the obvious vocabulary—**Thanksgiving, pilgrims, Indians,** and **feast**—children begin to develop their understanding of abstract words such as **customs** and **traditions**. They connect some important social studies place names to the pilgrims who crossed the **Atlantic Ocean** and landed at **Plymouth, Massachusetts**. They learn important geography terms if they locate England, Massachusetts, and the Atlantic Ocean on a **map** and a **globe**.

To introduce children to important economics concepts, many teachers transform their classrooms for a few weeks into a microworkshop. Children **manufacture** certain **products** or perform certain **services** and are paid **wages** for their **labor**. Abstract concepts such as **revenue, surplus, income,** and **taxes** are built into these classroom economic simulations.

Many elementary schools have student **governments**. **Elections** are held for the important **offices** of school **president** and **vice president**. Students in each class **vote** by secret **ballot** and **elect representatives** who become part of the school **legislature**. Some schools even have a **judicial council** that helps make school **rules** and determines how these rules will be **enforced** and **interpreted**.

When important **national** and **state elections** are being held, many schools hold mock elections. Students learn about the important **issues** and **vote** for the **candidates** of their choice. Because of their simulated experience in **democracy,** these students eagerly watch the results of the elections and compare the state and national results with the results at their schools.

In many schools today, fieldtrips are limited by tight budgets and liability concerns. The majority of fieldtrips taken by elementary children, however, are linked to the social studies curriculum. Walks to places in your school neighborhood can make the notions of communities, community helpers, and services clearer to your students. If a visit to your state's capital or our nation's capital is out of the question, could you visit the seat of local government? Would the mayor or city manager take a few minutes to lead a tour of your local municipal building and talk about the services provided by your local government? Do you have a local museum that you and your students could visit and use as a springboard to begin learning about the history of your community? When thinking about how you can provide real, concrete experiences to anchor social studies concepts, always consider what fieldtrip options you have.

Direct, hands-on experience with content-specific terms does not occur as naturally in social studies as it does in math and science. Knowing how important real experiences are to anchoring academic vocabularies, teachers and schools that are serious about maximizing vocabulary development in social studies seek ways to involve their students in simulations of the concepts and make the most of any possible fieldtrips. In classrooms that use simulations and an occasional fieldtrip, social studies comes alive, and student motivation and engagement are greatly increased.

Virtual and Visual Experience

When you can't provide real experience, look to your virtual and visual resources to anchor abstract social studies terms. Just as you can take virtual fieldtrips in science, your class can travel to distant places and back in time using the Internet and other computer resources. One of the original virtual fieldtrips and still popular in the fifth edition is *The Oregon Trail* (The Learning Company). In this game, students cross the country in a Conestoga wagon and test their wits against the weather and a variety of realistic misfortunes. This social studies simulation game was so popular that it now has several sequels, including *The Yukon Trail, The Amazon Trail,* and *The African Trail*. There are also a variety of economic simulation games, including *Lemonade Tycoon* (Hexacto) in which students set up a lemonade stand and try to make a profit. To succeed, they have to consider variables such as location, how hot the weather is, and how much of each supply to buy.

Perhaps you can't take a real fieldtrip to the White House or Plymouth Plantation or the Jamestown of John Smith, but through the Internet, you can make a virtual visit. Before investing your time and resources in a virtual fieldtrip, make sure it will be worth your while. Some sites have only pictures and text. Others have videos and interactive games to engage your students. *National Geographic* (www.nationalgeographic.com) is the source of many marvelous virtual fieldtrips. Africam (www.africam.com/wildlife) will take you to many beautiful parks in Africa where your students can view wildlife on the webcam.

Pictures and other visuals can help you build social studies concepts. Photographs that represent different historical time periods are particularly useful in helping children picture life in a world very different from their own. A picture file of digital images of important people and places is invaluable in anchoring social studies vocabulary. Google and other search engines have a "search image" function that makes it remarkably easy for you to compile your picture file.

Picture Walks in Social Studies

In Chapter 7, Picture Walks were suggested for introducing vocabulary before reading. Picture Walks are a very effective way to introduce vocabulary before students read a social studies selection in a textbook or other source such as a *Weekly Reader, Scholastic News,* or *Time for Kids* article. When you do a Picture Walk with students, you make use of the pictures in the selection to connect new words to old concepts and to build new concepts.

Social Studies Picture Books

A wide variety of picture books is another invaluable resource that directly or indirectly teaches social studies content and vocabulary. Picture books can transport you and your students to locations all over the world and back in time to historic moments. Abstract terms such as **segregation, prejudice,** and **equality** come to life if you share David Adler's *A Picture Book of Rosa Parks* with your students. **Democracy, constitution, independence,** and many other abstract terms become real to your students if you read them Maestro and Maestro's *A More Perfect Union: The Story of Our Constitution.*

Picture Books Build Social Studies Vocabulary

National Geographic publishes several series of books that help build social studies concepts. Its Travels Across America series includes *The Northeast, The Southeast, The Midwest, The Southwest,* and *The West*. Its Windows on Literacy Social Studies series includes *The Great Pyramid, The Story of the Pony Express, Race to the Pole,* and many other wonderfully illustrated titles. David Adler's picture biographies make history come alive. Titles include *A Picture Book of George Washington, A Picture Book of Harriet Tubman, A Picture Book of Jackie Robinson,* and *A Picture Book of Lewis and Clark*.

When looking for things to read aloud to your students that will help them build concepts, look beyond biography and other factual books to poetry and fiction. Many of the wonderful poems and stories enjoyed by elementary children have geographical and historical settings that help children learn about other times and cultures and anchor core social studies vocabulary. *The Way We Do It in Japan* by Geneva Cobb Iijima is a story of a boy and his family who move to Japan for a year and experience life in a very different culture. Many adults learned a lot of geography and historical concepts about the Plains by reading the *Little House on the Prairie* books by Laura Ingalls Wilder. Social studies is the part of the curriculum in which teachers help children develop their beginning understandings of history, geography, and culture. Books can indeed be your transport back in time and across the land and seas.

Preview-Predict-Confirm

In Chapter 5, I suggested that you could teach your students to predict vocabulary words they would meet during reading by showing them some visuals from a text they were about to read and having them predict words they would find in the text. The students work in trios to predict the words and then read the text to see which words actually occur. Here are the words one trio predicted after viewing some visuals from a *Time for Kids* article about the London Olympics.

England	arena	Queen Elizabeth
Thames	stadium	Kate
torch	buses	William
ceremony	badminton	champions
gold medal	**London Olympics**	world
underground	archery	USA
tennis	basketball	trains
athletes	soccer	police
volleyball	swimming	countries

After selecting one word they thought was common to all the groups—*England,* one word they thought was unique to their group—*archery,* and one word they were most interested in—*torch,* the trio read to see which words actually occurred. Next, they chose five or six words they wish they had thought of—*silver, bronze, wrestling, aquatics, rings, flame.* Finally, each student wrote two sentences, each of which included at least two of the words on their original list and words they wish they had thought of. Here are a few of their sentences.

Queen Elizabeth, William, Kate, and Harry took part in all the Olympics ceremonies.

There are 26 Olympics sports including volleyball, tennis, archery, soccer, basketball, aquatics, and wrestling.

The Thames River goes right through the middle of London.
The torch and flame are part of the opening and closing ceremonies.
Athletes can win gold, silver, and bronze medals.

Preview-Predict-Confirm (PPC) is a lesson format students love, and it teaches them how to use the pictures in a text to predict vocabulary they will meet. It also helps build new vocabulary as the trio members talk together about what they see and what things are called. Using the words in writing at the end helps solidify these words in their vocabulary stores.

Kid-Friendly Definitions

Chapter 7 contrasted dictionary definitions with kid-friendly definitions and suggested that although real, virtual, or visual experience is always required when introducing new words that are new concepts for your students, kid-friendly definitions could be used to introduce students to new words for concepts they already know. Imagine, for example, that the new vocabulary you wanted to teach in a unit on Communities included the words **past, present,** and **future**. You decide that most of your children have some concept for each of these words and just need to connect the new word to the old concept. You introduce each word with a student-friendly explanation and invite your children to share their connections with these words. The vocabulary introduction might sound something like this:

> "Boys and girls, we are going to be learning more about our community this week, and we are going to learn about how our community was different a long time ago when your grandparents were your age. We need to learn some new words to talk about the differences, and this is the first word I want you to think about."

(Teacher shows the students an index card with the word **present** written on it and has everyone pronounce **present**.)

> "Now I know you know one meaning for the word **present**. When would someone give you a present?"

(Kids eagerly share examples of getting presents for birthdays, Christmas, etc.)

> "Yes, we often get presents on our birthdays and other holidays. There is another meaning of **present** I want you to think about. **Present** can mean 'right now' or the time we are currently living in. Let me show you another word, and we will think about the difference between **present** and **past**."

(Teacher shows **past** on an index card. Kids pronounce **past,** and teacher reminds students of a meaning they may know for **past**.)

"Many of you know that I walk to school, and I walk past the library on my way here. Who else walks to school? What things do you walk past to get here?"

(Kids share examples of walking past the store, gas station, park, and other neighborhood landmarks.)

"**Past** has another meaning. **Past** can mean something that happened a long time ago. Most of you know that before I moved here, I lived in California. I could say that in the past, I lived in California. But in the present, I do not live in California. I live here."

(Teacher asks children who moved here from other places to share where they lived in the past.)

"So **present** means right now, and **past** is anytime before right now. Sometimes the past is a long time ago, and sometimes it is just a little while ago. But the past is always before the present. Now let me show you another time word."

(Teacher shows **future** on an index card.)

"This is the word **future**. Everyone say **future**. The future is a time that has not yet happened. I could tell you that my mom, who still lives in California, is thinking about moving here in the future. She is not presently here, but she may move here sometime later this year—in the future. Think of something that has not happened yet but you think will happen in the future."

(Children share examples of future events—including the impending birth of a baby sister, a planned trip to Iowa, and the retirement of a grandfather. Teacher shows all three index cards, has the students pronounce the words again, and expands the kid-friendly definitions.)

"So when we talk about what is happening right now, we call that time the **present**. If something happened before this time, we call that the **past**. Sometimes the past is just a little while ago, and sometimes the past is a long time ago. When something has not happened yet but we are waiting for it to happen, we say it will happen in the **future**."

With any type of vocabulary introduction, it is crucial that students have a chance to use the word for which the teacher has just provided an explanation. The easiest way to ensure that your students are actively involved in your vocabulary introduction is to seat them with a talking partner and have them "turn and talk." After providing your student-friendly explanations for **past, present,** and **future,** have students connect their experiences to these words by giving them a "turn and talk" task.

> "Turn and talk to your partner about something important happening right now in your life, something that happened in the past, and something you are looking forward to happening in the future. Be sure to use the words **present, past,** and **future** so your partner will know when the things you are talking about happened or will happen."

Give children a minute to talk and then ask them to tell something their partners told them. Prompt them to use the words **past, present,** and **future** in their sharing.

> "Paul, can you tell us something Manuel told you that happened in the past?"
>
> "Carla, can you tell us something Miguel told you that will happen in the future?"
>
> "Sharon, can you tell us something Kevin told you that is happening now, in the present?"

Even in social studies, where many of the words are new words for new concepts, some vocabulary words are simply new words for concepts your students already have. When you are introducing vocabulary such as **past, present,** and **future** that most of your students already have concepts for, you can give them kid-friendly definitions for those words and then provide an opportunity for them to connect each word to their experience by giving them a quick "turn and talk" task. If you regularly ask children to share what their partner told them, they will listen better to each other in anticipation of needing to share that information with the class.

Kid-Friendly Definitions and English Language Learners

Kid-friendly definitions are important for everyone, but they are critical for children who are learning English and for whom the terse definitions found in a dictionary are not at all informative. If you are having difficulty coming up with a kid-friendly definition for a social studies term, Vocabulary.com can probably help you.

My dictionary defined *abolition* as *an abolishing, as of slavery*. *Abolish* was defined as *to do away with something such as a law, institution, or custom; to put an end to, as in slavery*. At Vocabulary.com, I found a kid-friendly definition that explained that abolition was getting rid of something and gave examples of abolishing slavery, performance-enhancing drugs from sports leagues, and rats from cities. I use Vocabulary.com daily because they illustrate the meanings of words with memorable examples.

Maximizing Vocabulary Development with Multimeaning Words and Word Parts

The vocabulary you build during social studies will help your students build richer social studies concepts. Just as in other subject areas, some words you teach will have the same meaning in general use as they have in social studies. Other words have a social studies meaning and another different meaning. If students know the more general meaning of a term, that meaning can confuse them and interfere with comprehension when they are reading social studies content. Helping students access the more general meaning for the word and then explaining how the word has a different meaning in social studies can prevent confusion. For children who don't know the word's general meaning, your teaching of both meanings will help them add two new meanings to their vocabulary store.

Another way to increase vocabulary size when teaching social studies words is to draw students' attention to word parts—prefixes, suffixes, and roots. Whenever you teach vocabulary in any subject area, ask yourself whether there are other words that you could quickly teach your students by showing them the related words and talking about how the words are related. Here are just a few of the "bonus words" you could add to your students' vocabularies if you teach other meanings of a multimeaning word and capitalize on word parts.

Social Studies Word	Related Words	Other Meanings
border	borderless, borderline	
coast	coastline, coastal	coast down the hill coaster under a glass
continent	continental, intercontinental	Continental Airlines
direction	direct, director, misdirected	director of a play
east	eastern, easterly, southeast, northeast, mideast	
planes		airplanes
scale	scaly, upscale	scale that weighs things fish scales scale a mountain
consumer	consume, consumable	
competition	compete, competitive, competitor	
depression	depress, antidepressants	prone to sadness an indentation
prejudice	judge, judicial, judiciary, justice	
nation	national, nationality, nationalize, international, internationalize	
product	produce, producer, production, reproduce, reproduction	answer in multiplication
courage	courageous, encourage, encouragement, discourage	
rights	rightful	right answer right turn
responsibility	responsible, irresponsible	
economy	economical, economics	economy car
population	popular, overpopulated	
patriotism	patriot, patriotic	New England football team

Talking and Writing

After words are introduced in as vivid and rich a way as possible, students need opportunities to use these words as they talk and write. Students will eagerly discuss social studies words if their task is to List, Group, and Label; create word webs and concept maps; choose 10 important words; and categorize.

List, Group, and Label

Chapter 8 described how you could use a List, Group, and Label activity to help your students interact with and develop deeper meanings for math words. The List, Group, and Label activity format was actually developed to promote concept development in social studies. Here is how you could use List, Group, and Label to get your students speaking the new social studies vocabulary.

- Create a list of social studies words with which you want students to work. The list can include words only from a topic you are currently studying or it can include words from several topics.

- Form groups of three or four children and give them the list of vocabulary words you have chosen. Have them cut the words apart so that each child has an equal number of the words.

- Have the students work together to put words into groups that go together in some way. Once they have combined a group of words, they should come up with a name or label for that group.

- Appoint a recorder in each student group who will write down the group's words and their labels.

- Once each student group makes, labels, and records one group of words, have the children take back their words and create a new group. Students should come up with a label for this second group, and the recorder should record the group words and the label.

- If there is time, have the students create, label, and record a third group.

- When the allotted time is up—10 to 15 minutes—let each group of students share one of their word groups and tell what they called it.

- If there is time, have students choose one of the word groups they made and come up with other words not included on the list that belong in their group.

Here are some important social studies terms and how some students categorized the words into groups.

governor	nation	president	state	mayor
judge	ballot	past	town	city
Indians	community	country	future	county
pilgrims	urban	present	colonists	capital
rural	products	workers	suburban	council
leaders	election	tourism	factory	government

rural, urban, suburban; labeled "different parts of the county"
future, past, present; labeled "time words"
workers, leaders, colonists, pilgrims, Indians, governor, president, judge, mayor; labeled "people"
colonists, pilgrims, Indians; labeled "people who aren't here any more"
governor, government; labeled "words with govern as part of them"

List, Group, and Label is a simple but engaging way to get your students to think about important vocabulary and to talk with one another about the attributes of each word. Children enjoy creating the word groups. As they create the groups, they are talking with one another about the words and how they fit together. Many students particularly like the final activity in which they choose one of their groups and try to come up with words that were not on the list that belong in that group.

Word Webs

Your students can create vocabulary word webs by drawing a web with four to six spokes and filling the spokes by choosing from various word categories. On each spoke, students should put something that helps them remember the word. You may want to post a chart of some possible word web categories such as the one shown here for the word *frigid*.

Word: Frigid

Category	Example
1. Original Sentence (Copy the sentence containing the word.)	Pat was not used to the frigid weather conditions he now faced.
2. Dictionary Definition (What does the dictionary say the word means?)	extremely cold
3. New Sentence (Use the word in a sentence that shows what it means.)	A winter day at the North Pole would be frigid.
4. Closest Experience (When have you seen it?)	My aunt has a big freezer, and the inside of it is frigid.
5. Explanation of Meaning (In your own words, what does it mean?)	Frigid means very, very cold.
6. Main Idea (What is it?)	a way to describe temperature
7. Details (What are some parts of it?)	you can see your breath, ice and snow
8. Synonym (What words have nearly the same meaning?)	cold, freezing, polar
9. Antonym (What words have nearly the opposite meaning?)	warm, hot, burning
10. Word Family Members (What words share the same root, or base?)	Frigidaire, refrigerator, fridge
11. Visual (Illustrate the meaning of the word.)	

Be sure you make this a group activity because you want your students to "talk" the words as they decide which categories to include in their webs.

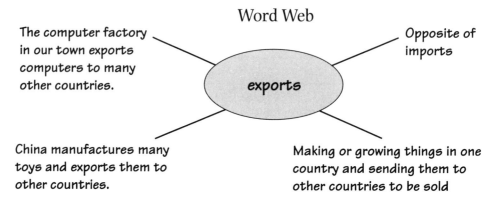

Word Web

The computer factory in our town exports computers to many other countries.

Opposite of imports

exports

China manufactures many toys and exports them to other countries.

Making or growing things in one country and sending them to other countries to be sold

Concept Charts

In social studies, we often help students learn about character traits such as responsibility, courage, and honesty. After the students have talked about these concepts, they can work in groups to create concept charts. Concept charts always include non-examples as well as examples that help students clarify an abstract concept.

Courage Concept Chart

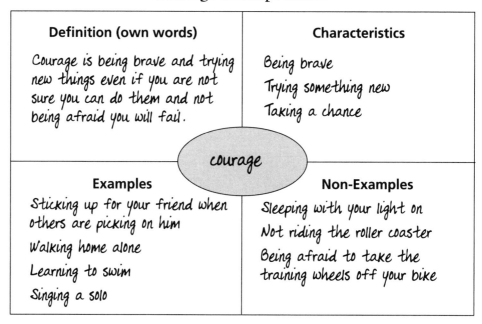

Definition (own words)	Characteristics
Courage is being brave and trying new things even if you are not sure you can do them and not being afraid you will fail.	Being brave Trying something new Taking a chance

courage

Examples	Non-Examples
Sticking up for your friend when others are picking on him Walking home alone Learning to swim Singing a solo	Sleeping with your light on Not riding the roller coaster Being afraid to take the training wheels off your bike

Categorize

For some topics, you may want students to review words by putting them into categories. Here are the categories and words one teacher chose for a selection on Japan.

Japan

Food	Geography	Products	Sports

Asia	sumo	ships	Pacific Ocean	karate
fish	automobiles	tea	soccer	rice
mountains	forests	baseball	textiles	soybeans
robots	noodles	islands	electronics	

Ten Important Words

Ten Important Words was described in the science chapter as a lesson format that helped children determine the most important words when reading in science. Identifying important words is equally important in social studies. Put your students in trios or quartets and have them read a short social studies selection together. Give them 10 sticky notes to place on what they decide are the 10 most important words. When the groups have read the selection and chosen the 10 words, make a class tally. The 10 words chosen by the most students become the 10 most important words for that selection and are listed in the order of the number of times the words were chosen. After reading a selection on Japan, one class compiled this list of the top 10 most important words.

1. Japan
2. Asia
3. Tokyo
4. islands
5. Pacific Ocean
6. automobiles
7. electronics
8. volcanoes
9. forests
10. soccer

Once the top 10 list is compiled, have each student write two sentences, each of which contains at least two of the words.

Social Studies Vocabulary for English Language Learners

Because many social studies terms are abstract, they present special problems for children who are learning English. Much of the academic vocabulary of social studies does not consist of just new words for known concepts. Both the concept and the word are apt to be unknown. Unlike many science and math words, you often cannot ask your English language learners to tell you the word for the new concept in their language because they lack both the word and the concept.

The difficulty of teaching social studies vocabulary to English language learners is further complicated by the fact that these students often lack the cultural referents many native English speakers have for the words. Children who associate Florida with Disney World® and New York with the New York Yankees have some kind of starting point for thinking about these states, the northeast, the southeast, and the Atlantic Ocean. Using as much real, virtual, and visual experience as possible and providing varied opportunities to use new vocabulary in talking and writing is important for all vocabulary learning. Assuring these multiple, interactive encounters with social studies words is essential for your English language learners.

Teaching the Academic Vocabulary and Language of Social Studies

Look again at all the core social studies vocabulary included in the lists in this chapter. Where are your students going to learn these words if they don't learn them during your social studies instruction? A few of these words—**workers, holiday, family**—occur in the everyday language of all your students. Other words—**honesty, traditions, election**—occur in the everyday language of some children whose parents have higher levels of education. Many of these words—**region, scarcity, imports**—do not occur in everyday language anywhere. Think about the television programs your students watch and the movies they see. Think about the books they choose to read. Social studies, like all subject areas, has an academic vocabulary that children must learn. Much social studies vocabulary is abstract. Providing your students with multiple real, virtual, visual, speaking, and writing encounters with the academic vocabulary of social studies will result in greater social studies learning and increases in both the size and depth of your students' vocabularies.

chapter 11

Building Vocabulary While You Teach Art, Music, and PE

To truly make vocabulary development a priority, you must seize every opportunity across the school day to expand and enhance your students' vocabularies. This chapter explores some often-overlooked vocabulary development opportunities in the gym, on the playground, and in the art and music rooms. Just as for other curriculum areas, your first step toward maximizing vocabulary growth during art, music, and physical education is to create a list of core words for these topics. To develop this list, I consulted Marzano's (2004) Physical Education, Arts, Theatre, Dance, and Music lists and the curriculum standards of several states for these areas. Consider these lists as starting points for developing your own list.

Physical Education

ability	endurance	offense	skate
activity	equipment	opponent	skiing
amateur	exercise	pass	skill
athlete	field	physical	skipping
balance	fitness	player	slide
baseball	flexibility	practice	soccer
basketball	football	procedure	softball
catch	gallop	professional	sport
challenge	game	race	sportsmanship
championship	goal	racket	stretch
climb	gymnasium	recreation	strike
coach	gymnastics	referee	swimming
competition	hockey	relay	tennis
course	hopping	rink	throw
court	jogging	rules	track
cycling	jump	running	training
defense	kick	score	umpire
diving	league	shoot	winners
dribble	movement	sideline	

Music, Dance, and Drama

actor	drums	musician	role
applause	duet	orchestra	scale
audience	entertain	percussion	scenery
band	guitar	performance	solo
bass	harmony	performer	song
cast	horn	piano	soprano
clapping	instrument	pitch	stage
composer	keyboard	play	strings
conductor	lighting	production	tempo
costume	march	props	tenor
dance	melody	recorder	theater
drama	music	rhythm	voice

Visual Arts

artist	contrast	kiln	perspective
brush	crayon	materials	scissors
camera	draw	medium	sculpture
canvas	easel	museum	texture
clay	exhibit	oil	tools
color	gallery	paint	watercolor

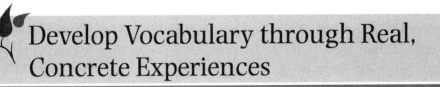

Develop Vocabulary through Real, Concrete Experiences

As you look at the lists, do all the opportunities for real, hands-on experiences jump out at you? If social studies contains the largest number of abstract words and concepts, the arts and physical education contain the largest number of concrete words. Your students "do" most of these words: They sing and dance and jump and draw and paint. The things they don't do are things they touch, hold, and use—such as basketballs, paintbrushes, and recorders—or things they help create—for example, scenery and costumes. There are a few abstract terms—**rules, harmony,** and **perspective**—but these abstract terms can quickly be connected to concrete experiences.

One very potent reason for spotlighting vocabulary during art, music, and physical education is that the most powerful way to learn new words is the essence of what these curriculum areas are all about. You don't need to contrive any real experiences; you just need to capitalize on them and draw attention to the words that name and describe the activities. The challenge for you in developing vocabulary as you engage your students in art, music, and physical education activities is that vocabulary development opportunities are so obvious that you will overlook them! That is why developing your core vocabulary lists for these areas is so important. Post your list somewhere where you will glance at it often. As you lead your students in activities, be sure you use all the appropriate words and give your students opportunities to use them. Write the words on index cards, as you do for other subject areas, and have your students pronounce the words and use them with one another.

Before going to the playground, for instance, show the students the word **equipment** and ask them what equipment the physical education helpers need to carry to the playground. Take a few seconds to expand the meaning of **equipment** by asking them what equipment is needed for various tasks, such as cooking, fishing, and camping. Ask them to "turn and talk" to a partner about some activity they do on the weekend and what equipment they use for that activity.

Before giving out instruments for your rhythm band, show students the word **instruments**. Have them pronounce the word and then name the instruments used in the rhythm band. Ask the children to name any instruments they know about that are not rhythm band instruments. Do they know anyone who plays the guitar? The drums? The piano? Where have they seen an organ? A keyboard? Ask them to think about their favorite instrument and why it is their favorite. Then have them "turn and talk" to their partner about their favorite instrument.

As you begin your art activity, show students the words **medium** and **materials**. Talk about the different materials that are used in art and the different mediums (media) they have worked in this year. Show them the materials they will use today and what medium they will work in. Give the children just a minute to imagine that they grow up to become great artists and decide which materials and mediums they will be famous for. Then ask them to "turn and talk" about their artistic aspirations.

Real experiences are what art, music, and physical education are about. You don't need to contrive the experiences to teach the vocabulary—you just need to make sure you don't miss the opportunity!

Develop Vocabulary through Virtual and Visual Experiences

In addition to being musicians, artists, and athletes, most people are spectators at these events. Discuss with your students how people go to **galleries** and **museums** and see **exhibits** by a variety of **artists** using a variety of **media**. If taking your students on a fieldtrip to a gallery or museum is not feasible, could you set up an exhibit and transform your classroom or halls into a gallery? PBS and the Discovery Channel produce some excellent videos that you can use to take your students on virtual fieldtrips to see the greatest art all over the world (http://www.googleartproject.com/). As you and your students take these virtual voyages, be sure to seize all the vocabulary development opportunities, including learning the names of the most famous artists, the names of places where they created their art, and where that art is displayed.

Would it be possible to take your students to a concert? Would your local high school band come to your school and put on a concert for your students? Are there any musicians on your faculty or school staff who shouldn't give up their day jobs but who could put on a concert for your students? If you can't arrange any kind of real musical event for your students, you could surely find some video footage of bands and orchestras. Be sure you connect all the vocabulary words possible to whatever musical experiences you arrange for your students to watch. In addition to the obvious words—**musician, orchestra, band, conductor, concert,** and names of instruments—seize the opportunity to develop other concert-related words such as **audience, applause, intermission,** and **solo.**

Could you take your students to a sports event? Perhaps a local intramural game? Can you use a video of a game to build sports-related vocabulary? Look at the list of physical education vocabulary and imagine the possibilities for developing vocabulary, including vocabulary that is not just sports-specific—for example, **competition, endurance, defense, offense,** and **professional**.

In addition to engaging your students in doing art, music, and physical education, you have numerous opportunities to engage your students as spectators for art, music, and sports events. Make the most of these virtual and visual opportunities to develop arts- and sports-specific vocabulary as well as vocabulary with more general use. Most kids love art, music, and physical education. If you connect vocabulary development to these activities, some of that positive affect might translate into more positive attitudes toward words!

Use the Arts to Promote Vocabulary Growth for English Language Learners

Have you noticed that there are no language barriers when your students participate in art, music, and physical education activities? Take advantage of the "level playing field" all your students are on during these activities to spotlight vocabulary. All students will benefit, and your English language learners will absorb the words as they participate fully in the activities.

Capitalize on Student Enthusiasm for Art, Music, and PE to Teach Word Parts

Look again at the lists that began this chapter. Many of the words—even the simple, common words—have word parts used in other (and often more complex) words. Simple words such as **jog, dance, skate, paint,** and **drum** can be used to teach the **er** meaning that transforms these simple words into **jogger, dancer, skater, painter,** and **drummer.** **Actor** and **conductor** can be used to demonstrate that sometimes **or** at the end of words indicates a person who does the action. Here are some words for which you can help your students build meaning by demonstrating how many other words are related to art, music, and physical education words.

Arts/Physical Education Words	Bonus Words
jog/dance/skate/paint/drum, and others	jogger/dancer/skater/painter/drummer and others
ability	able, unable, inability, disability
activity/actor	act, active, inactive, action, react, reaction, counteract
athlete	athletic
competition	compete, competitive, competitor
cycling	bicycle, tricycle, unicycle, motorcycle, cyclist
defense/offense	defend/offend, defensive/offensive
endurance	endure, unendurable
flexibility	flex, flexible, inflexible, reflex
sportsmanship/championship	friendship, fellowship
composer	compose, composition, decompose, decomposition
conductor	conduct, conduction

(continued)

Arts/Physical Education Words	Bonus Words
entertain	entertainer, entertainment
harmony	harmonious, harmoniously, disharmony
production	produce, producer, reproduce, reproduction
scenery	scene, scenic
exhibit	exhibition, exhibitor
color	coloring, discolored, colorize, watercolor
field	outfield, infield, fielder, fieldhand
movement	move, movers, immovable
drama	dramatic, dramatize
sculpture	sculptor

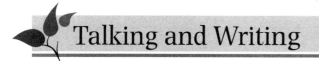

Talking and Writing

In spite of the fact that most art, music, and physical education words are easily connected to real, virtual, and visual experiences you are providing, students still need to use the words to own them. Students would enjoy categorizing some of these words in a List, Group, and Label format.

artist	brush	canvas	draw	paint
contrast	kiln	clay	sculpture	perspective
sculptor	camera	color	crayons	easel
materials	medium	museum	gallery	watercolor
exhibit	texture	scissors	tools	oils

sculptor, artist; labeled "people who do art"
museum, exhibit, gallery; labeled "places you see art"
easel, paint, brush; labeled "equipment you need to paint with"
clay, kiln; labeled "things you need to make pottery"

Or perhaps the students could complete a data chart contrasting some sports.

	Basketball	Football	Baseball	Hockey	Tennis
Equipment					
Positions					
Number of Players					
Team Name					
Actions/ Movements					
Scoring					

Students could also write cinquains about their favorite sport, musical instrument, or artist.

Basketball

Shoot   baskets

Dribbling,   passing,   jumping

Bounces   off   the   rim

Victory!

Perhaps most consistent with the nature of art, music, and physical education, your students could pantomime words and have the class guess the word they are dramatizing. Imagine the fun your students will have and the good discussion that will go on as they work in groups to plan pantomimes for this list of words:

gymnastics	coach	defense	tennis
referee	equipment	relay	softball
dribble	flexibility	stretch	
balance	offense	winners	

Use Art, Music, and PE to Maximize Vocabulary Learning in Your Classroom

Most of us have never thought about using art, music, and physical education as a venue of vocabulary development. When you think about the importance of providing real, virtual, and visual experiences to anchor words and when you consider students' enthusiasm for these subjects, the vocabulary connection seems obvious. In fact, I hope you will conclude as I have concluded: "How not?"

chapter 12

Word Wonder

Making vocabulary instruction and activities as engaging and lively as possible has been one of my top priorities in writing this book. Children enjoy listening for the words in Three Read-Aloud Words and getting to shout, "Stop! *Catastrophe*!" when you read a

text where **catastrophe** occurs. They are intrigued by the sports articles you read to them and use to engage them in thinking about word parts. Their eyes are riveted to the board as you slowly write the letters of a word and they try to be the first one to guess the word you are writing. Introducing vocabulary with real, virtual, or visual experiences is important not only because this kind of experience is how children learn words best but also because they respond enthusiastically to these experiences. Working with classmates to put words in groups, create word webs, and plan pantomimes are social opportunities most children enjoy. Promoting a "Words Are Wonderful!" attitude has been a hidden agenda throughout this book because, ultimately, the attitudes your students develop toward vocabulary will determine how many new words and meanings they add to their vocabulary stores. Most of the new words students acquire as they go through school will be words they meet in their reading and the ones they develop meanings for using pictures, context, and word parts. It is not enough to know how to figure out the meanings of new words that are encountered while reading. The children have to want to do it! In addition to the suggestions in previous chapters for making vocabulary instruction as engaging as possible, here are some other suggestions for promoting word wonder.

Model Your Own Word Wonder during Teacher Read-Aloud

Reading aloud to your students every day is critical to vocabulary growth because children who are exposed to lots of wonderful and various books and magazines are motivated to do more independent reading. You can get more vocabulary mileage from your read-aloud time if you stop occasionally and marvel at the author's wonderful word choice.

In *Bridge to Terabithia,* Katherine Paterson (1977) describes a happy feeling as "joy jiggling inside" (p. 101). Pausing for just a moment, rereading the phrase, and marveling at how the words let you feel what the characters are feeling help your students become aware of the power of words and how great authors choose words to paint pictures and bring readers into the story. In addition, each time you stop, reread, and marvel, you are demonstrating to your students that you think words are truly wonderful.

Some books call special attention to words by presenting them in humorous or unusual ways. Countless children have delighted in Amelia Bedelia's literal attempts to dress a chicken and draw the drapes. *Donavan's Word Jar* (DeGross, 1994) is a story about a boy who becomes fascinated with words and starts collecting unusual ones by writing them on slips of paper and sticking them in his word jar. Many teachers read this book to their students and then present their students with word jars for their word collections. In other classrooms, the class has a word jar. Children who find words so good they don't want to forget them jot them down on a colored strip of paper, initial them, and put them in the jar. From time to time, the words in the jar get dumped out, and the person who contributed that word explains why it is such a wonderful word.

The classic read-aloud book that teachers use to promote word wonder is Norton Juster's *The Phantom Tollbooth* (1961). With the Spelling Bee, the watchdog Tock, and the Humbug, Milo, the book's main character, journeys through Dictionopolis, feasting on square meals and synonym buns. Older elementary children delight in this fantasy and find the word play truly awesome. Sharing books with children that celebrate and play with words is just one more way to show your students that you are a genuine word lover.

Classroom Word Jar

Model Choosing Wonderful Words for Your Budding Authors

After modeling your wonder at the awesome words authors choose to paint pictures and put the reader right into the action, capitalize on your students' enthusiasm for "just the right word" by modeling how they, as authors, can use truly awesome words in their writing. Teach some mini-lessons in which you use boring, common, not-very-descriptive words in your first draft and then, noticing these "tired" words, revise your draft by replacing the "dead" words with more "lively" ones.

Don't tell the children your intent ahead of time. Just write a piece as you normally write during a writing mini-lesson. When you finish your draft, have the class read it with you and ask them whether they can think of any ways you can make your writing even better. If no one suggests replacing some of your "overused" words, you will need to suggest it yourself.

"I notice that I have some common words here that don't create very vivid pictures. **Good,** for example, doesn't even begin to describe how wonderful the cookies were. I think I will cross out **good** and replace it with **scrumptious**."

Continue replacing some of your boring, overused, or inexact words, eliciting suggestions from your students about which words need replacing and what words to use in replacing them.

Once you have modeled replacing boring words with more lively words in several mini-lessons, ask your students to try this revising strategy in one of their pieces. Have them work with partners as you circulate, giving help as needed. When they have had a few minutes to revise, select a few good examples of revision to share with the whole class.

"Show, don't tell" is a basic guideline for good writing. Unfortunately, many children (and adults) are not sure what this guideline means. To teach your students what it means, you have to practice what you preach and *show* them how to "Show, don't tell" instead of taking the far easier road of *telling* them to "Show, don't tell"!

To teach children to replace "telling" words with words and sentences that "show," write some pieces in which you purposely tell rather than show and then revise these pieces in mini-lessons with the children's help. You might also want to use paragraphs from some of your students' favorite authors as examples and rewrite these by replacing the showing words with telling words and sentences. After identifying the places where your students wish the writer had shown them rather than told them, read the original to them and compare the "telling" version with the "showing" version. After several mini-lessons, partner your students and ask them to help each other find examples in their own writing where they could make the writing come alive by replacing some of their telling words with showing words and sentences.

Use "Stuff" to Build Vocabulary and Promote Word Wonder

Everybody likes stuff! Look around your house or apartment and identify common objects your students might not know the names of—even if they have the same objects in their houses! Here are some of the objects one teacher brought to school for "show and talk."

vases—assorted sizes, colors, and shapes

balls—tennis ball, baseball, basketball, football, golf ball, volleyball, and beach ball

art—watercolors, oils, and photographs in frames of different colors, materials, and sizes

kitchen implements—turkey baster, strainer, spatula, whisk, and zester

tools—hammer, screwdriver, nails, screws, drill, and wrench

In addition to the names of objects, of course, lots of descriptive words are used in talking about what you do with the objects. You may want to engage your students in a game of 20 Questions, in which you think of one of the objects and they see how many questions they have to ask you to narrow down which one it is.

In addition to gathering objects from home and carting them to school, look around your school environment and think about what objects your students might not know the names for. They probably know the words **door** and **window,** but can they tell you that what goes around the door and window is the **frame**? Can they tell you that the "things" that allow the door to open and close are the **hinges** and that the thing you grab to open and close the door is the **knob**? They can turn the water in the sink off and on, but do they know that they use **faucets** to do that? Is your playground covered with **asphalt**? **Gravel**? **Grass**? **Sand**? What kind of **equipment** do you have in your **gymnasium** and what can you do with it?

Many of the objects you bring to school or identify in school to build vocabularies can also be found in your students' home environments. Get into the habit of posing questions that will send students looking for and identifying similar objects in their homes.

- Do you have tools (kitchen implements, balls, vases, picture frames, etc.) in your house? What do they look like? What do you use them for?

- How many faucets (hinges, knobs, ledges, door frames, etc.) do you have in your house? Count them and bring in the number tomorrow. We will add up all the numbers at the beginning of math.

- Is there gravel (asphalt, grass, sand, etc.) anywhere in your neighborhood?

- Is there a playground or park near your house? What kind of equipment does it have?

In addition to having children identify common objects in their home environments, encourage them to talk with family members about these. "Tell your family that we have these at school, too, and what these things are for. Tell them about how we are using batteries—like the ones you have at home—to learn about electricity."

Teachers are always looking for opportunities to make home–school connections. Having children take new vocabulary words they are learning into their home environments helps make school learning more relevant and extends each child's opportunities for vocabulary development.

Encourage Your Students to Build Word Collections

Kids like to collect stuff—baseball cards, rocks, shells, and stickers, to name just a few. Find ways to enable your students to collect words and provide opportunities for them to share their collections with other collectors. This chapter began with suggestions for promoting word wonder in your teacher read-alouds by including books in which words are cherished. Collecting words in a jar, just as Donavan did in *Donavan's Word Jar,* is a simple way to motivate all your students to collect words.

Another simple way to establish the routine of word collecting is to have one child contribute a word to the One Wonderful Word board each day. Divide one of your bulletin boards into spaces for each student. Make each space large enough to display a large index card and label each space with each child's initials. Include a space for yourself. Each day, working in order across and down the board, one child places an index card with his or her "wonderful word" and explains why he or she chose that word. Depending on the age of your students, you may want to specify a minimum number of letters the word must have. If you like, you can also let the designated child choose three words added by other children and explain why she or he likes these words, too. When you and all the children have had a turn, begin the rotation again and have each child tack the second word on top of the first word. If you begin

One Wonderful Word				
Mrs. C outstanding	AC chimpanzee	GH precarious	PJM persistent	DM drawbridge
BE generous	TW expedition	KB ridiculous	JD environment	PLM emergency
AM hibernate	RA immigrants	SJM generation	BJ firecrackers	ZC victorious
RS explorers	PD performers	JH video games	SAM delicious	JM championship
DC invention	KC brontosaurus	DH impressive	CH revolution	KL frustration

this early in the year, your students will have been introduced to 150 or more words that their classmates think are wonderful! More importantly, your students will always be on the lookout for a wonderful word so they can impress everyone with their choice. Establishing and maintaining a One Wonderful Word board takes minimal time and preparation, but it pays big dividends by keeping the notion of wonderful words front and center in your classroom.

Many teachers like students to keep vocabulary notebooks. If you do this, make sure your students see themselves as word collectors rather than definition copiers. In fact, most teachers do not allow students to copy any definitions into their notebooks. Rather, the students include the sentence in which they found the word and a personal connection with the word. Students often enjoy illustrating the words in their collections with pictures and diagrams. Some older word sleuths like to include some information about the word's origin.

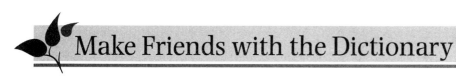

Make Friends with the Dictionary

Think back to your elementary school days and recall your associations with the word **vocabulary**. Do you remember looking up words and copying their definitions? If the word had several definitions, did you copy the first one or the shortest one? Did you ever look up a word and still not know what the word meant because you didn't understand the meaning of other words in the definition? Did you copy that definition and memorize it for the test in spite of not understanding it? Do you remember weekly vocabulary tests in which you had to write definitions for words and use these words in sentences?

Copying and memorizing definitions has been and remains the most common vocabulary activity in schools. It is done at all levels and in all subjects. This definition copying and memorizing continues in spite of research that shows definitional approaches to vocabulary instruction increase children's ability to define words but have no effect on reading comprehension (Baumann, Kame'enui, & Ash, 2003). Beck, McKeown, and Kucan (2002) sum up the damper that typical dictionary activities can put on word wonder:

> Becoming interested and aware of words is not a likely outcome from the way instruction is typically handled, which is to have students look up definitions. Asking students to look up words in the dictionary and use them in a sentence is a stereotypical example of what students find uninteresting in school. (p. 12)

There are, however, a variety of ways to promote active use of the dictionary that help students broaden their concepts and also teach them what a valuable resource the dictionary is. Students should learn to turn to the dictionary when they need a precise definition of a word. A teacher who regularly says, "Let's see what the dictionary can tell us about this word," and sends one child to look it up models the way adults who use the dictionary actually use it. (Did you ever see an adult look up a word to copy and memorize the definition? Maybe the reason so few adults use dictionaries is because that is the only way they ever saw anyone use it!) If you have a dictionary on your classroom computers, model how useful it is by asking a child to "see what our computer dictionary has to say about this word."

In many classrooms, helpers are appointed to jobs each week. Someone greets visitors and waters the plants. Why not appoint a weekly Dictionary Disciple? This person gets possession of "the book" and is always ready to be dispatched to the farthest corners of the wide world of words to seek and share facts about words.

Another activity students enjoy that teaches them how to use dictionaries authentically is based on the notion of semantic gradients (Greenwood & Flanigan, 2007). As described in an article in *The Reading Teacher,* semantic gradients are used to help students discern shades of meaning. Students are given a gradient with two opposites placed on each end. One example from this article has the gradient bounded by **despondent** and **euphoric**.

Despondent _____ **Euphoric**

Students are provided a word box from which they choose words to place along the gradient. For **despondent** and **euphoric,** the example words in the word box are **happy, elated, unhappy, glum,** and **sad.** Students work in groups to place these words along the gradient from **despondent** to **euphoric**. The completed gradient might look like this:

despondent glum sad unhappy happy elated euphoric

Students then come together as a class to share their thinking in deciding where to place the words. The authors suggest that students become good at completing a gradient when they progress through a series of steps. First, they have a box of words to choose from; then they can be given the gradient with the extreme examples of the opposites; and finally, without the help of a word box, they come up with words and place them along the gradient.

I am quite taken with the semantic gradient idea because I think children would enjoy talking about the words and trying to decide what shades of meaning they have, but I worry that many children would not have enough knowledge of the shades of meaning to make reasonable decisions. I have adapted this activity to allow the students to use a dictionary and thesaurus in making their decisions. The adaptation makes the task more "do-able" for more students and provides authentic experiences with the dictionary and thesaurus. I call this activity Rank Opposites. In Rank Opposites, students use a dictionary to help them decide where to put the boxed words. Once students become more sophisticated at using the dictionary to decide where to place the boxed words, they are no longer given any boxed words. Rather, they use a thesaurus to determine which words to add and where to place them. Depending on the age and vocabulary sophistication of your students, you can vary the format, type, and number of words used. Here are some Rank Opposites variations.

One variation is to give the students the extremes placed on the continuum and six to eight boxed words. Students use dictionaries to find the words, read the definitions together, and decide where to place the words.

wail _____ guffaw

laugh	giggle	whimper	smile
sob	cry	chuckle	frown

petrified _____ fearless

fearful	timid	afraid	courageous
daring	terrified	brave	valiant

sizzling _____ frigid

cold	lukewarm	hot	cool
warm	frosty	scorching	chilly

In another version, you place the common opposites on the gradient and students decide where to place the others, including the extremes.

_____ big _____ little _____

colossal	huge	tiny	miniature
enormous	gigantic	small	mammoth

	like ____ dislike		
hate	despise	adore	worship
loathe	love	detest	enjoy

Another possibility is to place one word in the center and then have students place other words to show some variation on this word.

	said		
whispered	yelled	murmured	mumbled
shouted	screamed	hollered	

	walk		
scurry	saunter	stroll	sprint
dash	run	meander	mosey

After students learn how to use the dictionary and determine shades of meaning, you can help them learn to use a thesaurus by providing them with the basic words but no box of words. Students brainstorm words they know with similar meanings and then look up these words in a thesaurus to come up with other examples. Given the common opposites **wet** and **dry,** students might construct a gradient that looks like this:

drenched   soaked   soggy   damp   wet   dry   arid   parched   waterless

Given the extreme opposites **wealthy** and **destitute,** students might use the thesaurus to construct this gradient:

wealthy   prosperous   affluent   well-off   rich   poor   broke   penniless   destitute

Given the common word **wonderful,** students might construct this gradient:

good   nice   pleasant   great   wonderful   splendid   fantastic   magnificent   awesome

For all Rank Opposites lessons, it is important for students to work in small groups to determine the words and the ranks. Remember that "talking the words" is one of the major avenues for claiming ownership of new vocabulary. When students are using shades of meaning to rank words, they will not always be in agreement. What is important is not the exact order of the words but that students are talking and thinking about shades of meaning. Be sure to communicate to your students that their thought and discussion about where to place the words—not the exact placement—is what matters.

Digital Dictionaries Support English Language Learners

It is neither quick nor easy to find a word in a paper dictionary or thesaurus. When working with digital resources, meaning and pronunciation help is often just a click away. E-readers have built-in dictionaries. All children make more use of the dictionary when it is digital, but this support is particularly helpful for English language learners. Enchanted Learning (EnchantedLearning.com) has an extensive picture dictionary that provides the word in several languages, including Spanish, French, Japanese, and Portuguese.

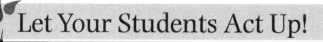

Let Your Students Act Up!

Word dramatizations are powerful ways to help students build vivid word meanings. Both skits and pantomimes can be used to help students "get into words." To prepare your students to do vocabulary skits, select six words and write them on index cards. Tell your students that in a few minutes, their group will plan a skit—a quick little play—to demonstrate the word they have been given. Choose a few students to work with you and model for them how to plan a skit. Talk with your group as the rest of the class listens in. Plan a scene in which you can use the word several times. When you have a plan, act out your skit using the target word as many times as possible. Have one member of your group hold up the word every time it occurs in the skit.

Imagine, for example, that the word your group is acting out is **curious**. You decide that the skit will involve a dad and his 2-year-old walking to the post office. The dad and the toddler meet several people on their walk, and each time, the 2-year-old stops, points to the stranger, and asks questions:

"What's your name?"

"Where are you going?"

"What's that?"

"What are you doing?"

"What's in the bag?"

"Why are you wearing that funny hat?"

The dad smiles each time and explains to the stranger that his son is curious about everything. The strangers answer the boy's questions and then remark, "He's the most curious kid I ever saw," as they walk on.

Perform the skit as the class watches. At the end of the skit, have the people in the skit ask the audience how the skit showed that the little boy was curious. Finally, ask whether anyone in the audience has a story to share about a curious person.

Next, assign the class to five groups, putting one of the children who helped in the skit in each of the groups. This child gives each group a card on which the word the group will dramatize is written. Today, the teacher is focusing on adjectives and has given the groups the words **nervous, frantic, impatient, jubilant,** and **serene**. The groups plan their skits with a little help from the teacher, who circulates around and coaches them. As she hoped would happen, the teacher sees that the child in each group who helped in the model skit is taking a leadership role and helping boost the group's confidence that they can do this.

Each skit is acted out with one person in each group holding up the card each time the word is used. The group then asks the audience what they saw in the skit that made the word "come alive." The teacher asks whether anyone in the class wants to share a personal experience with the target word. After the last skit, the teacher places the six word cards with others on a board labeled "Get Your Adjectives Here! Cool Describing Words to Spice Up Your Talk and Writing."

Another form of dramatization is pantomime, which is particularly useful when the words you want to teach are emotions or actions.

Imagine that you want to introduce the emotional adjectives **confused, disappointed, furious,** and **frightened**. A pair of students can be assigned to each word. The rest of the class watches the pairs pantomiming the words and tries to guess which pair is acting out each word. The same kind of pantomime can be done with actions, such as **swaggered, crept, sauntered,** and **scurried**. Adverbs are fun to pantomime. Imagine four pairs of students walking to school. One pair walks **briskly**. One pair walks **cautiously**. One pair walks **proudly**. One pair walks **forlornly**.

For any kind of dramatization, it is important to conclude the activity by asking all the students to relate the word acted out to their own experience:

"When have you been confused? Disappointed? Furious? Frantic?"

"When have you swaggered? Crept? Sauntered? Scurried?"

"When would you walk briskly? Cautiously? Proudly? Forlornly?"

Acting out words in skits and pantomimes provides students with real experience with words. They remember these words because of this real experience and because they enjoy acting and watching their friends act. Keep a list of words your class encounters that could be acted out in skits or pantomimes and schedule 20 minutes for vocabulary drama each week. You will be amazed at how their vocabularies and enthusiasm for words will grow.

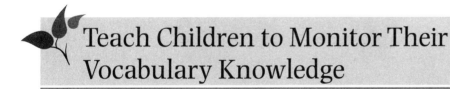

Teach Children to Monitor Their Vocabulary Knowledge

One of the first steps in learning anything is recognizing that you don't already know it. Children need to notice when they come to words they don't have meanings for. Sometimes, young children get so focused on pronouncing new words that they fail to realize they don't know what it means. Children can be taught to self-assess their vocabulary knowledge using a simple scale like this one:

1 = I never heard of that word.

2 = I heard the word, but I don't know what it means.

3 = I think I know what that word means.

4 = I'm sure I know what that word means.

5 = I can make a good sentence with that word.

This scale could be used with any of the activities for teaching vocabulary. To make this quick and easy, consider using a five-finger, every-pupil-response system. Say the word you are focusing on and ask everyone to show you the appropriate number of fingers. When you are focusing on words for the first time, be sure that you positively acknowledge all the responses so that children don't get in the habit of showing you five fingers

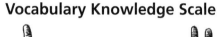

Vocabulary Knowledge Scale

"I never heard of that word."

"I heard the word but I don't know what it means."

"I think I know what that word means."

"I'm sure I know what that word means."

"I can make a good sentence with that word."

just so they "look good." Try acknowledging their vocabulary self-assessment with comments such as these:

> "I see lots of one and two fingers. That makes me happy because I know I chose a word you need when I chose **desperate**. **Desperate** is an important word and lots of you don't know it yet."

> "Some of you think you know the meaning of **desperate,** and some of you are sure you do. Can someone tell me what you think it means?"

> "I see someone with five fingers up. Todd, tell me your sentence that shows the meaning of **desperate**."

After you have worked with the new vocabulary words for several days, ask the children again to show you how well they know the meanings of these words and comment on how many people are showing four or five fingers. Many teachers display a chart such as the one shown here to help children remember the five-finger vocabulary self-assessment system.

Play Games

Kids love games, and there are a lot of wonderful word games. Camille Blachowicz and Peter Fisher (2004) have developed a wonderful list of possible games. Here is my adaptation of their list:

- *Match, Go Fish,* and *Old Teacher:* Match is a card game like Concentration in which children pick up cards and take them if they have a "match." Children can construct the cards to go in the game. Match can be used to review vocabulary words taught in any area, and the cards can match in different ways. Matching cards could be a picture and the word that goes with the picture (*buffalo, giraffe, peacock*); synonyms in which one word is a "tired, overused word" and the other word is a more vivid word (*happy, joyous; said, shouted; shook, trembled*); or antonyms (*even, odd; large, small; less, more; above, below*). Cards are turned over and then placed back in the same spot if they do not match.

If a player gets a match, he or she takes the pair and has another turn. When all the cards have been taken, the person with the most cards is the winner. The same deck of cards that was created for Match can be used to play Go Fish. Add a card with a drawn picture of an "Old Teacher" and play a variation of Old Maid. Kids choose cards from one another and match pairs. The person left with the Old Teacher loses!

- *WORDO:* Choose nine words and tell the students to write them in different places on their WORDO sheet. Give definitions for words. If students have the word that matches the definition, they cover the word. The first person with a row or column covered wins!

- *Commercial Games:* Many commercial word games are appropriate for classroom use, particularly with intermediate-aged children. Popular commercial word games include Scrabble, Probe, Pictionary, Boggle, and Outburst. Newer word games are always being developed, so be on the lookout and be the first classroom in your hall to have the new, hot game!

- *Crossword Puzzles:* There are many books of simple crossword puzzles that your children will enjoy solving. Have them work together with a partner or in a trio to ensure lots of talk about the words. Several Internet sites allow you to download crossword puzzle-creating programs. Older children enjoy creating crossword puzzles with unit or story vocabulary. Let everyone work in small groups to create a puzzle and then let other groups solve the puzzles.

- *Computer Word Play:* Many Internet sites provide a variety of word-play games and activities. Just search for word play or word games and you will find some sites that are particularly appropriate for your students.

Use Word Humor

A man sits down at a bar and orders a club soda. He hears a soft voice say, "My, you are a handsome man." He looks around and does not see anyone else at the bar. He picks up his drink and hears, "That shirt is a good color on you." The voice seems to be coming from a bowl of nuts at the end of the bar. He calls the bartender over and tells him he thinks he is hearing voices. The bartender says, "It's the nuts. They're complimentary!" (paraphrased from Stahl & Nagy, 2006, p. 147)

Many jokes, like this one, turn on the meaning—or in this case, the two different meanings—of a word. All children enjoy jokes, even the corny jokes. Using jokes in your classroom will promote your students' "words are wonderful" attitude and provide everyone a much-needed moment of comic relief. Jokes are everywhere.

Riddles are another kind of word humor. There are numerous sites on the Internet with jokes and riddles appropriate for elementary children.

Promote Word Wonder

Enthusiasm is contagious! Teachers who are enthusiastic about words project that enthusiasm by conveying their eagerness to learn unfamiliar words and by sharing fascinating words they encounter outside the classroom. Young children are usually enthusiastic about new words, repeating them over and over, enjoying the sound of language and marveling at the meanings being expressed. Encourage the continuation of this natural enthusiasm. Open your class to wondering about words, to spontaneous questions about unfamiliar words, to judgments about the sounds and values of words. Make engaging activities like the ones described in this book a regular part of everyday life in your classroom, and your students will conclude that words are indeed wonderful!

Book Study Guide
for
What Really Matters
in Vocabulary

Book Study Guidelines

Many schools now are organized in professional learning communities (PLCs) because they recognize the power of collaborative learning. Book studies often play a large role in helping PLCs reflect upon and achieve best practices. The intent of a book study is to provide a supportive context for accessing new ideas and affirming best practices already in place. Marching through the questions in a lockstep fashion could result in the mechanical processing of information; it is more beneficial to select specific questions to focus on and give them the attention they deserve.

One possibility for structuring your book discussion of *What Really Matters in Vocabulary* is to use the Reading Reaction Sheet on page 240. Following this format, make a copy for each group member. Next, select a different facilitator for each chapter. The facilitator will act as the official note taker and be responsible for moving the discussion along. He or she begins by explaining that the first question is provided to start the group discussion. The remaining three questions are to be generated by the group. The facilitator can ask each person to identify at least one question and then let the group choose the three they want to focus on, or the facilitator can put the participants into three groups, with each group responsible for identifying one question. The three questions are shared for all to hear (and write down), and then discussion of Question 1 commences. The facilitator paces the discussion to bring out the most relevant information for that group. Since many school districts require documentation for book studies, the facilitator could file the sheet with the appropriate person as well as distribute a copy to all group members for their notes.

Another possibility is to use the guiding questions for each chapter. You could have the same facilitator for all chapters. Perhaps this would be someone who read the book first and suggested it to the group. Or the facilitator role could rotate. The facilitator should not only pace the group through the questions to hit on the most important information for the group's needs, but he or she should take notes for later distribution to group members and/or administrators if required for documentation.

The provided questions are meant to provoke discussion and might lead the group into areas not addressed in the questions. That is wonderful! The importance of a book study is to move the members along in their understanding of the book content. If time is limited, the facilitator might select certain questions from the list for the initial focus of the discussion, allowing other questions as time permits.

Of course, a third option is to combine the two structures. Select the format that best fits your group and the timeframe you have set for completion of the book.

All book sessions should end with a purpose for reading the next chapter. It could be to generate questions the group still has, to find implications for each person's own teaching, or to identify new ideas. Purpose setting is a time-honored way to help readers (of any age) approach the text. If you are using the questions that accompany each chapter, direct the participants to read the questions prior to reading the chapter. This will provide a framework for processing the information in the chapter.

Book Study Questions for Each Chapter

chapter 1: Why Vocabulary Matters

1. Pat Cunningham opens the book by describing her personal experiences teaching children with limited vocabularies. Compare your teaching experiences with hers. Can you cite specific examples of vocabulary gaps for children you have taught?

2. Pat describes how she used teacher read-aloud, pictures, and real objects as daily activities to build meaning vocabulary. How do you use these three activities to build vocabulary? Can you think of ways to enhance your use of read-alouds, pictures, and objects to maximize vocabulary growth?

3. Did you realize that determining vocabulary size is such a complex task? Talk with your group about how you think vocabulary size should be determined.

4. Are you a "word" person—someone who loves to learn new words and notices words in everyday life? How do you know? How do you develop word wonder among your students? What do you think the role of word wonder is in developing vocabulary?

5. This chapter lays out seven principles for teaching vocabulary. Talk about each of these principles. Which ones do you and your colleagues do well? Which ones could you do more of?

6. How many of your students are English language learners? What specific things do you do to adapt your instruction to accommodate the vocabulary needs of your students who are learning English?

7. Look at all the Common Cores State Standards (CCSS) that relate to meaning vocabulary. What do they tell you about the crucial link between vocabulary and reading, writing, speaking, and listening?

8. The chapter ends with a description of a fifth-grade classroom's yearlong effort to implement a comprehensive vocabulary effort. What impressed you about the vocabulary growth of these children from a low-income school? Perhaps one of

your group members could read the article and provide more details about how the teacher provided rich and varied language experiences, taught individual words, taught word-learning strategies, and fostered word consciousness.

9. Generate a question that this chapter raised for you. Bring it to the group for discussion.

chapter 2: Reading Is What Matters Most!

1. This chapter begins with a justification for the chapter title "Reading Is What Matters Most!" by describing the relationship between how much you read and the size of your vocabulary. Share personal examples of students who read a lot and had large vocabulary stores and students who read little and had small vocabulary stores. Are you convinced that reading is what matters most?

2. Document your students' reading using the "Me and Reading" tool or some other assessment. What did you find out about the amount of reading your students are doing? Does that amount vary for your good readers and struggling readers?

3. Do you read to your class at least once each day? Does your read-aloud include both fiction and nonfiction? Do you read some "everyone" books—books that the most struggling readers in your classroom could read? If you have English language learners, do you choose some books to read-aloud specifically for their vocabulary development potential? How can you maximize the effects of your teacher read-aloud?

4. Do your students read materials of their own choosing each day? Do your struggling readers actually read for most of the allotted time? What works and what is difficult about the independent reading time in your classroom?

5. Do you confer with your students about their independent reading? Would any of the conference suggestions in this chapter make your conferences more efficient, informative, and enjoyable?

6. What are the ways you have your students share and talk about books? Would any of the suggestions in this chapter help you find the time for sharing? What other ideas does your group have for structuring the sharing and finding the time to fit it in?

7. What strategies from this chapter do you see yourself using? Why?

8. Generate a question that this chapter raised for you. Bring it to the group for discussion.

chapter 3: Tell Your Students to Talk!

1. Do your students love to talk? Would you like to turn this natural affinity for talking into more productive talk? Is talking in your classroom a bane or a boon?

2. This chapter suggests many ways to incorporate "turn and talk" opportunities in your classroom routine. Which of these ways do you currently use? Which could you adapt and include? What other ideas does your group have for using "turn and talk" to increase the amount of productive talk students engage in?

3. Think-Pair-Share is a variation of "turn and talk" you may want to consider if your children "talk before they think." How might this variation work better for your students?

4. Structured discussions are another opportunity for students to talk. They usually take more time than the partner talking and the groups that include three or four students. Which of the structured discussion formats do you think would be more useful to your students? For which parts of your curriculum would you use the different formats?

5. In some classrooms, certain children "hog" all the time and do all the talking. If this is a problem in your classroom, consider using the Numbered Heads Together or Jigsaw Groups formats. How do these two formats hold everyone in the group accountable?

6. If you teach some children who are learning English, talk with your colleagues about how partner talk and structured discussions would help them learn English. Whom would you partner up or place in the same group with your English language learners?

7. Language Standard Three of the CCSS requires that students learn how to participate in discussions. How would the suggestions in this chapter help your students meet this standard?

8. What strategies from this chapter do you see yourself using? Why?

9. Generate a question that this chapter raised for you. Bring it to the group for discussion.

chapter 4: Writing Builds Expressive Vocabulary

1. How many of your students like to write? Using new words in writing is one of the most important activities your students can do to actually "own" the words. Because writing is complex and hard, many students (and teachers!) don't do much writing. Discuss your students' attitudes toward writing. How would sneaking some quick-writes into your day make writing less onerous?

2. Think-Write-Pair-Share accomplishes the same goals as Think-Pair-Share with the bonus that your students do some extra "painless" writing. Which of these two formats would work best with your students? Can you find places for both of these if you think across your entire day and all the different subjects you teach?

3. The author asserts that you won't do quick-writes very often if you have to wait on everyone to get out paper and pencils. She suggests that you keep recycled paper scraps and special pens handy for students to use for their quick-writes. Would that work in your classroom? What other ways can you think of to get the quick-writes done in the time it would take everyone to find paper and pencils?

4. The chapter describes Two-in-One True Sentences, Journals, Cinquains, A Ticket Out the Door, and Top Three Things I Learned This Week as versatile quick-write formats. Which of these would fit into your classroom routines? When and in what subjects would you be most likely to use them?

5. If you teach some children who are learning English, talk with your colleagues about how quick-writes would help them learn English.

6. What strategies from this chapter do you see yourself using? Why?

7. Generate a question that this chapter raised for you. Bring it to the group for discussion.

chapter 5: Teaching Vocabulary Independence

1. When your students are reading on their own, do you think some of them "skip it" when they come to a word they don't immediately recognize? Discuss with your colleagues why the "skip it" habit may be a huge roadblock to vocabulary growth.

2. Were you surprised by all the compound words or words with prefixes, suffixes, or endings added in the "Underdogs Win Championship" article? Can you see how recognizing these word parts and knowing what they mean would enable your students to figure out pronunciations and meanings for words they might currently be skipping? How "morphologically sophisticated" are your students?

3. Chapter 2 cited research and common sense to support the fact that most of the new words you learn are learned from reading. Context and morphology are the two clues that allow you to figure out the meanings of unfamiliar words. Talk about how you used context and morphology to figure out many of the words in the technology paragraph. Could you do a similar demonstration with your students to convince them of the power of context and morphology?

4. Have you ever been reading with one of your students and had them stop at a new word, such as *kangaroo,* and look to you for help when there was a kangaroo pictured? Did you point to the picture, ask them the name of the animal, and get the response, "a kangaroo"? Pictures are the other clue, along with context and morphology, that help readers figure out an unfamiliar word. Many struggling readers don't use the picture clues to help them identify words. Preview-Predict-Confirm (PPC) is a lesson format specifically designed to teach your students to

make maximum use of picture clues. How would this lesson format fit into your instruction? Which students do you think would profit most from learning to "mine the graphics" before reading the text?

5. One of the reasons some of your students may have developed the "skip it" habit is that they don't know how to use the text to figure out the meaning of an unfamiliar word. Three Read-Aloud Words allows you to teach them this critical independent word-learning strategy. If students are in the habit of skipping words, however, they may continue to do this when reading on their own, even when they have learned how to figure out meanings. Word Detectives and Sticky Note Day are intended to help them "kick" the "skip it" habit. If you suspect that some of your students have the "skip it" habit, try these three interventions and share with your group how well they worked with your students, particularly with your struggling readers.

6. If you teach English language learners, discuss how these independent word-learning strategies will promote their vocabulary growth.

7. What strategies from this chapter do you see yourself using? Why?

8. Generate a question that this chapter raised for you. Bring it to the group for discussion.

chapter 6: Morpheme Magic

1. Compound words are a good place to begin your morphology instruction because they are everywhere and your students can usually figure out how the meaning of the compound word is related to the meanings of the words that make up the compound. Even first-graders can use compound words and are quite impressed with themselves when they can read big words such as *basketball, Thanksgiving, grandmother,* and *playground*. Look at a list of compound words (available on many Internet sites) and decide which ones would be most appropriate for the grade levels represented in your group.

2. Prefixes are the next easiest morphological unit to teach. They are always at the beginning of the word and don't change the pronunciation of the word as suffixes do. Students like hunting for words that begin with the prefix letters and sorting them into categories of Prefix (*dislike, disagree*) and Not Prefix (*dishpan, district*). Look at the prefixes in this chapter and decide at which grade level you would teach each and expect students to master them. If you teach older children, you may want to post the list of common prefixes and challenge them to find less common prefixed words in their reading (*antifreeze; contradict; bicycle*) and figure out the meanings of these prefixes.

3. Some of the suffixes (**er, est, ful, less**) are easy to understand and don't change the pronunciation of the word. Other suffixes are harder to understand, have

a variety of spellings, and change not the meaning of the word but how it can be used in the sentence. (The *explorers* went west to *explore* new places and their *explorations* showed what a vast and varied country we have.) Help your students see how they can use context and morphology together to decide how the meaning changes. Decide at which grade level in your school your students should master each of the common suffixes. If you teach older children, you may want to post the list of common suffixes and challenge them to find less common suffixed words in their reading (*freedom, asteroid, backward*) and figure out the meanings of these suffixes.

4. Were you surprised at the number of common cognates in English, Spanish, and French? How can you use cognates to help your students build their English vocabularies? How will you teach them to beware of false cognates?

5. Do a cost–benefit analysis for teaching your students Greek and Latin roots. Compare how much time it will take with how many word meanings your students will actually be able to figure out using these. If you teach English language learners, discuss how these independent word-learning strategies will promote their vocabulary growth. The roots in the chart on p. 107–108 are most useful. Are there others you think your students should learn?

6. What strategies from this chapter do you see yourself using? Why?

7. Generate a question that this chapter raised for you. Bring it to the group for discussion.

chapter 7: Building Vocabulary While You Teach Reading

1. The chapter begins by asserting that traditional vocabulary instruction during reading, which usually involves writing and memorizing definitions, is not very effective. It asks the question, "How many children who didn't already have these words in their meaning vocabularies will add these words based on these traditional activities?" What do you think? How effective is the traditional vocabulary instruction in actually teaching new word meanings during reading?

2. How does being "picky" with the words you choose mesh with preselected words from your reading program? Discuss the author's suggestion that you choose "Goldilocks" words that are essential for students to understand the big ideas in what they are reading. How will you choose the words on which you will focus your precious reading instructional time?

3. Instead of traditional vocabulary instruction, the author suggests that you consider introducing words with real, concrete experiences, take your students on virtual fieldtrips, and make maximum use of pictures and other visuals. How practical is this suggestion? Take a list of words you have selected to teach and

decide how many of them you could teach using these real, virtual, and visual experiences. Share the results of your assessment with your group.

4. For some words for which real, virtual, or visual experiences are not possible, consider kid-friendly definitions. Look the words up in a traditional dictionary and at Vocabulary.com. How would kid-friendly definitions make it more likely that your students would actually add these words to their vocabulary stores?

5. Use Rivet to introduce some words to your students. How do they respond to this lesson format? How are they talking and writing the words? What would you change the next time you use the Rivet lesson format?

6. The author ends the chapter with the radical suggestion that you "dump" traditional vocabulary instruction during reading lessons. What do you think? Can you replace the traditional dictionary definition copying and memorizing activities with real, virtual, visual experiences, kid-friendly definitions, and Rivet activities? What do your colleagues think? Has the time come for you to move on to vocabulary instruction during reading that has a better chance of actually increasing your students' vocabularies?

7. What strategies from this chapter do you see yourself using? Why?

8. Generate a question that this chapter raised for you. Bring it to the group for discussion.

chapter 8: Building Vocabulary While You Teach Math

1. Chapter 1 laid out seven principles for effective vocabulary instruction. The first and most important principle is that vocabulary is learned best when it is based on real, concrete experience. Math is the subject area in which manipulatives and concrete experiences play the most important role. Talk about the real, concrete experiences you can provide your students during math, including using the students as your manipulatives. How can you be sure to tie the critical math vocabulary to these experiences?

2. The second principle for effective vocabulary instruction is that pictures and other visuals help solidify word meanings. How do you use pictures and other visuals to help your students "own" the mathematics vocabulary you are teaching them?

3. The third principle is that to truly own a word, you must use that word in talking and writing. Chapters 3 and 4 described various talking and quick-write activities. This chapter includes math-specific talking and writing activities. How would these fit into your math instruction? What other ways have been successful in getting your students to speak and write math vocabulary?

4. Using your mathematics text and state or district standards, list the vocabulary students must know to understand the mathematical concepts at your grade level.

Circle the words that have different meanings in other content areas so you can make connections for your students. Star the words that have helpful word parts (prefixes, suffixes, roots). Do any of these words have cognates that would help your English language learners? Share your word lists with your book club group and decide which words students should master at each grade level.

5. What strategies from this chapter do you see yourself using? Why?

6. Generate a question that this chapter raised for you. Bring it to the group for discussion.

chapter 9: Building Vocabulary While You Teach Science

1. Science is the other subject area in which concrete, hands-on experiences play an important role. Talk about the real, concrete experiences you can provide your students during science. How can virtual fieldtrips make the science concepts seem real? How can you be sure to tie the critical science vocabulary to these experiences?

2. The second principle for effective vocabulary instruction is that pictures and other visuals help solidify word meanings. How do you use pictures and other visuals to help your students "own" the science vocabulary you are teaching them?

3. Look at the books (and magazines) you typically read aloud to your students and the books (and magazines) you have available in your classroom library. Find the ones that relate to science topics. Bring these to the next book club group and share how you use these with your students. (If you can't find many examples, consider how you could obtain more informational science materials for teacher read-aloud and independent reading.)

4. This chapter includes science-specific talking and writing activities. How would these fit into your science instruction? What other ways have you been successful in getting your students to speak and write science vocabulary?

5. Many elementary children have difficulty sorting out important ideas from trivial and interesting details. In information text, the key words also represent the important ideas. Try Ten Important Words with an upcoming reading selection in your science text or other material. At the next book club meeting, describe the lesson and what you learned while doing it.

6. Find a short text on the Internet that you plan to have your students read. Copy and paste it into WordSift (www.wordsift.com) and see which content-related words occur most often. How could you use this tool to help your students determine and learn meanings for important science words?

7. Using your state or district standards, list the vocabulary students must know to understand the science concepts at your grade level. Circle the words that have

different meanings in other content areas so you can make connections for your students. Star the words that have helpful word parts (prefixes, suffixes, roots). Do any of these words have cognates that would help your English language learners? Share your word lists with your book club group and decide which words students should master at each grade level.

8. What strategies from this chapter do you see yourself using? Why?

9. Generate a question that this chapter raised for you. Bring it to the group for discussion.

chapter 10: Building Vocabulary While You Teach Social Studies

1. What are the implications for social studies vocabulary instruction if, as Cunningham states, these words are "replete with abstract concepts"? How did you learn the meanings of abstract words like *citizenship* and *interdependence*?

2. Simulations, virtual fieldtrips, and visuals can help make abstract concepts less abstract. Discuss how you use them to help your students develop social studies concepts and vocabulary.

3. Many of us learned abstract concepts like "freedom," "community," and so forth from reading about those concepts in historical fiction books. Search for some historical fiction that fits your social studies curriculum. Bring the results of your search to share with your group.

4. Decide with your book club group some vocabulary words that are particularly difficult for your students to understand. Enter these words at Vocabulary.com. Discuss how the kid-friendly definitions and visuals help.

5. Try Ten Important Words with an upcoming reading selection in your social studies text or other material. At the next book club meeting, describe the lesson and what you learned while doing it.

6. What talking and writing activities from this and other chapters could you use to get your students speaking and writing social studies vocabulary? Can you think of other ways to get your students talking productively and engaging in quick-write activities?

7. Using your social studies text and state or district standards, list the vocabulary students must know to understand the social studies concepts at your grade level. Circle the words that have different meanings in other content areas so you can make connections for your students. Star the words that have helpful word parts (prefixes, suffixes, roots). Do any of these words have cognates that would help your English language learners? Share your word lists with your book club group and decide which words students should master at each grade level.

8. What strategies from this chapter do you see yourself using? Why?

9. Generate a question that this chapter raised for you. Bring it to the group for discussion.

chapter 11: Building Vocabulary While You Teach Art, Music, and PE

1. One of the wonderful things about a vocabulary focus during art, music, and physical education is that typically students view instruction differently in these content areas. Often there is more movement, greater use of specialized equipment, and a more relaxed stance. Teachers can take advantage of that atmosphere to focus on vocabulary. Discuss the pros and cons of this perspective.

2. Try some of the real, visual, talking, and writing activities in this chapter. Share your successes with your group and with any specialists who teach art, music, and PE to your students. What other ways can you think of to capitalize on student interest in these special subjects to maximize vocabulary development?

3. Using your art, music, and PE state or district standards, list the vocabulary students must know to understand these concepts at your grade level. Circle the words that have different meanings in other content areas so you can make connections for your students. Star the words that have helpful word parts (prefixes, suffixes, roots). Do any of these words have cognates that would help your English language learners? Share your word lists with your book club group and decide which words students should master at each grade level.

4. What strategies from this chapter do you see yourself using? Why?

5. Generate a question that this chapter raised for you. Bring it to the group for discussion.

chapter 12: Word Wonder

1. Have you created a "word wonder" classroom? How do you know? What do you do? Would your students say that you love words?

2. Do you have a favorite word-play activity or book? Share the activity or book with the group and explain why and how you use it.

3. Which of the activities in this chapter have you used regularly? Why? What was your students' response?

4. Is the learning justified for the amount of time word-wonder activities take? Discuss the issue of pressure for achievement versus learning to enjoy word study.

5. In the questions for Chapter 1, you were asked whether you are a "word" person. Has your answer to that question changed here at the end of the book? Why?

6. Generate a question that this chapter raised for you. Bring it to the group for discussion.

Reading Reaction Sheet

Facilitator/Recorder (person who initiated the discussion): _____

Group reactants: _____

_____

Date of reaction/discussion: _____

Chapter title and author(s): _____

_____

Question #1: What ideas and information from this chapter could be used in classroom instruction?

Reactions:

Question #2: _____

_____

Reactions:

Question #3: _____

_____

Reactions:

Question #4: _____

_____

Reactions:

References

Anglin, J. M. (1993). *Vocabulary development: A morphological analysis. Monographs of the Society for Research in Child Development, 58* (10, Serial #238).

Artley, S. A. (1975). Good teachers of reading—Who are they? *The Reading Teacher, 23,* 285–303.

Baumann, J. F. (2009). Vocabulary and reading comprehension. In S. E. Israel & G. G. Duffy (Eds.), *Handbook of research on reading comprehension.* (pp. 323–346). New York, NY: Routledge.

Baumann, J. F., Kame'enui, E. J., & Ash, G. E. (2003). Research on vocabulary instruction: Voltaire redux. In J. Flood, D. Lapp, J. R. Squire, & J. M. Jensen (Eds.), *Handbook of research on teaching the English language arts* (2nd ed., pp. 752–785). Mahwah, NJ: Erlbaum.

Baumann, J. F., Ware, D., & Carr Edwards, E. (2007). "Bumping into spicy, tasty words that catch your tongue": A formative experiment on vocabulary instruction. *The Reading Teacher, 61,* 108–122.

Beck, I. L., McKeown, M. G., & Kucan, L. (2002). *Bringing words to life.* New York, NY: Guilford.

Biemiller, A. (2004). Teaching vocabulary in the primary grades. In J. F. Baumann & E. J. Kame'enui (Eds.), *Vocabulary instruction* (pp. 28–40). New York, NY: Guilford.

Blachowicz, C. L., & Fisher, P. (2004). Keep the "fun" in fundamental: Encouraging word awareness and incidental word learning in the classroom through word play. In J. F. Baumann & E. J. Kame'enui (Eds.), *Vocabulary instruction* (pp. 219–238). New York: Guilford.

Clay, M. M. (1991). Introducing a new storybook to young readers. *The Reading Teacher, 45,* 264–273.

Common Core State Standards. Retrieved from http://www.corestandards.org/

Cummins, J. (1994). The acquisition of English as a second language. In K. Spangenberg-Urbschat & R. Pritchard (Eds.), *Kids come in all languages: Reading instruction for all students* (pp. 36–62). Newark, DE: International Reading Association.

Frayer, D., Frederick, W. C., & Klausmeier, H. J. (1969). *A schema for testing the level of cognitive mastery.* Madison, WI: Wisconsin Center for Educational Research.

Graves, M. F. (2004). Teaching prefixes: As good as it gets? In J. F. Baumann & E. J. Kame'enui (Eds.), *Vocabulary instruction* (pp. 81–99). New York, NY: Guilford.

Graves, M. F. (2006). *The vocabulary book*. Newark, DE: International Reading Association.

Greenwood, S. C., & Flanigan, K. (2007). Overlapping vocabulary and comprehension: Context clues complement semantic gradients. *The Reading Teacher, 61,* 249–254.

Hart, B., & Risley, T. (1995). *Meaningful differences in the everyday lives of young American children.* Baltimore, MD: Paul H. Brookes.

Hayes, D. F., & Ahrens, M. (1988). Vocabulary simplification for children. *Journal of Child Language, 15*(2), 395–410.

Ivey, G., & Broaddus, K. (2001). Just plain reading: A survey of what makes students want to read in middle school classrooms. *Reading Research Quarterly, 36,* 350–377.

Juel, C., Biancarosa, G., Coker, D., & Deffes, R. (2003). Walking with Rosie: A cautionary tale of early reading instruction. *Educational Leadership, 60,* 12–18.

Kagan, S. (1994). *Cooperative learning.* San Clemente, CA: Kagan Cooperative.

Lehr, F., Osborne, J., & Hiebert, E. H. (2004). *A focus on vocabulary.* Honolulu, HI: Pacific Resources for Education and Learning.

Manning, G. L., & Manning, M. (1984). What models of recreational reading make a difference? *Reading World, 23,* 375–389.

Marzano, R. J. (2004). *Building background knowledge for academic achievement.* Alexandria, VA: Association for Supervision and Curriculum Development.

National Clearinghouse for English Language Acquisition. (2011). *The growing numbers of English learner students, 1998/99-2008/09.* Washington DC: Author.

National Council for the Social Studies. (1994). *Expectations of excellence: Curriculum standards for social studies.* Washington, DC: Author.

National Council of Teachers of Mathematics. (2000). *Principles and standards for school mathematics.* Reston, VA: Author.

National Research Council. (1996). *National science education standards.* Washington, DC: National Academy Press.

Palmer, B. M., Codling, R. M., & Gambrell, L. B. (1994). In their own words: What elementary children have to say about motivation to read. *The Reading Teacher, 48,* 176–179.

Shefelbine, J. (1990). Student factors related to variability in learning word meanings from context. *Journal of Reading Behavior, 22,* 71–97.

Smith, Deb. (2001). My "high risk" students love reading real books. In P. M. Cunningham & D. P. Hall (Eds.), *True stories from four blocks classrooms* (pp. 23–32). Greensboro, NC: Carson-Dellosa.

Stahl, S. A., & Nagy, W. (2006). *Teaching word meanings.* Mahwah, NJ: Erlbaum.

Taba, H. (1967). *Teacher's handbook for elementary social studies.* Reading, MA: Addison-Wesley.

U.S. Census Bureau (2010). *American fact finder.* Washington, DC: Author.

Yopp, R. H. & Yopp, H. K. (2004). Preview-Predict-Confirm: Thinking about the language and content of informational text. *The Reading Teacher, 58,* 79–83.

Yopp, R. H., & Yopp, H. K. (2007). Ten important words plus: A strategy for building word knowledge. *The Reading Teacher, 61,* 157–160.

Index